AROUND BRUGES IN 80 BEERS

80

Second Edition

CHRIS POLLARD
SIOBHAN MCGINN

Cogan & Mater

Contents

Key to symbols

⓪ Place number

🍷 Café

✖ Restaurant

✉ Hotel

🛒 Shop

⊗ Closed days

🕐 Opening times

🍷 Number of beers

🍴 Food

Published by Cogan & Mater Limited.

© Cogan & Mater Limited 2009.

Managing Editor: Tim Webb

First Published 2006
Second Edition 2009

Printed in the United Kingdom at the University Press, Cambridge.

Book design: Dale Tomlinson
Typeface: OT Versa *(by Peter Verheul)*
Map: John Macklin
All photographs: Pollard & McGinn, with extra photos supplied by Filip Geerts, Inge, John White, Hans Golsteyr Patricia Segers and Antony Raes. Thanks also to Teresa Lang, Marc Struyf and Danny Van Tricht.

ISBN 978 0 9547789 4 1

Welkom!

BRUGES is one of Europe's top weekend destinations and for many visitors their first taste of Belgium. It attracts around three million visitors every year from all over the world and is particularly handy for visitors from Britain, being only an hour from either Calais or Brussels.

The visitors come to enjoy a splendidly preserved medieval city, famed for its architecture, lace and chocolates. However, it is also a great place to sample the diverse offerings of Belgium's finest brewers. How many other cities can offer 80 hugely different places selling 80 different top quality beers?

In 2006, after many years of visiting and drinking in the city we decided it was time to share our knowledge and point people to the cafés, restaurants and shops that stock the best beers. Thus the first edition was born. Three years on, things around Bruges have changed, with many new beer venues opening and some sadly gone. Bruges may look like a city set in the Middle Ages, but it is certainly dynamic on the beer front. This second edition features twenty-five new places and nearly half of the beers featured are new to the guide.

Around Bruges in 80 Beers is aimed at the general traveller who knows that Belgian beer is supposed to be good and wants to know where they can try the best, in the most interesting surroundings.

We have matched each of our 80 chosen places with a specific beer from their menu. The places we have chosen range from specialist beer shops to posh restaurants, from locals' bars to elegant taverns and from early risers to late night haunts. We even have a boat.

We have included beers from old family-run breweries, tiny new micro-breweries and some that will be like nothing you have ever tasted before.

There is no end to the places where you can drink dull, factory-made, brand name lagers from global producers with huge advertising budgets. We hope we can lead you away from these towards beers of exceptional quality, some little known outside Belgium, or in some cases the area where they are brewed.

Use our book to dig a little deeper and be more adventurous in your beer choices and to experience some of the truly exceptional offerings of this, the greatest brewing nation in the world. You will find out with practice, which beer styles and which beers you prefer.

And if 80 proves a bit too much for even a long weekend, we may just persuade you to return, again and again.

We hope you enjoy reading, and more importantly, using this book as much as we enjoyed researching it.

CHEERS!

Podge & Siobhan

Listings

BEER SHOPS

② 2be
⑤ Bacchus Cornelius
⑧ Bier Tempel

HOTELS AND HOSTELS

④ Atelier – Hotel Kempinski (★★★★★
⑥ Bauhaus (★) and Hostel
㉗ Erasmus (★★★)
㉛ Ganzespel – Nicky's B&B
㉟ Gran Kaffee de Passage
㊹ Krakele (★★)
㊽ Pergola – Die Swaene (★★★★)
㊿ Snuffel (BUDGET)
㊾ Verdi – B&B

CAFÉS WITH GREAT BEER LISTS

① @ The Pub (86+)
⑮ Brugs Beertje (250)
⑰ Cambrinus (400)
㉔ Dickie's (80+)
㉗ Erasmus (125)
㉜ Garre (130)
㊶ Kelk (195+/–)
㊺ Kuppe (100)
㉶ Poatersgat (110)

Restaurants

- **4** **Atelier** (MODERN FLEMISH)
- **6** **Bauhaus** (EUROPEAN)
- **9** **B-In** (MODERN EXOTIC)
- **10** **Bon Vivant** (GRILLS)
- **11** **Bottelier** (MODERN FLEMISH)
- **13** **Bretoen Pannenkoeken** (PANCAKE HOUSE)
- **14** **Bron** (VEGETARIAN)
- **16** **Cafedraal** (MODERN FLEMISH)
- **17** **Cambrinus** (BISTRO)
- **19** **Celtic Ireland** (IRISH EUROPEAN)
- **20** **Cookies** (TAPAS)
- **22** **Curiosa** (BISTRO)
- **23** **Dell'Arte** (BISTRO)
- **24** **Dickie's** (GRILLS)
- **26** **Dyver** (BEER CUISINE)
- **27** **Erasmus** (BEER CUISINE)
- **31** **Ganzespel** (BISTRO)
- **33** **Gezelleke** (BISTRO)
- **34** **Goldies** (BISTRO)
- **35** **Gran Kaffée de Passage** (CLASSIC FLEMISH)
- **36** **Gruuthuse Hof** (CLASSIC FLEMISH)
- **43** **Kluiver** (BISTRO)
- **47** **Lamme Goedzak** (CLASSIC FLEMISH)
- **49** **Lokkedize** (GREEK)
- **50** **Marieke Van Brugghe** (CLASSIC FLEMISH)
- **51** **Meridian 3** (VARIED)
- **52** **Nieuw Museum** (GRILLS)
- **57** **Oude Speye** (VARIED)
- **59** **Pallieterke** (FLEMISH)
- **60** **Panier d'Or** (FISH)
- **62** **Pergola** (MODERN FLEMISH)
- **63** **Pietje Pek** (TRADITIONAL FLEMISH)
- **65** **Republiek** (WORLD)
- **66** **Ryad** (MOROCCAN/INDIAN)
- **70** **Strijdershuis** (CLASSIC FLEMISH)
- **74** **Veloren Hoek** (BISTRO)
- **75** **Verdi** (FRENCH/BELGIAN)
- **79** **Zandloper** (FLEMISH)

Specials

- **2** **2be** (BELGIAN PRODUCE SHOP)
- **6** **Bauhaus** (INTERNET)
- **19** **Celtic Ireland** (LIVE MUSIC)
- **30** **Fiore** (KITSCH)
- **37** **Halve Maan** (BREWERY)
- **40** **Jerry's** (CIGAR BAR)
- **46** **Lamme Goedzak** (BOAT)
- **53** **Nieuwe Tempelier** (ARCHERY)
- **56** **Origin'O** (ORGANIC SHOP)
- **77** **Vlissinghe** (ANCIENT)
- **80** **Zwarte Kat** (MUSEUM)

Late drinking

- **1** **@ The Pub**
- **12** **Bounce**
- **25** **Druid's Cellar**
- **29** **Ezeltje**
- **49** **Lokkedize**
- **54** **On The Rocks**

5

Kriek
A lambic in which cherries have been steeped for six months to create a sweet and sharp drink, the cherry taste in which may be anywhere from subtle to intense. Poor quality cherry beers use fruit syrup and are more like lager and blackcurrant in taste and in principle.

Dubbel
The Flemish Dutch word for double, implying double malt in the brew and so double strength. Usually a brown ale of 6–8%, often with allusions to monks or abbeys and sometimes made to raise money for same.

Lambic
Collective term for the beer styles made from beer fermented using wild yeast found in the atmosphere, which land on

the freshly brewed liquid while it is cooling. Traditional lambics are fermented in oak casks for one to three years and used mainly for blending to make *gueuze* (above) or steeping with fruit.

Gueuze
Traditional (*oude*) gueuze is made from blending two or more lambics (below) and adding a tiny amount of sugar to spark refermentation while it lies in the cellar in champagne-style bottles. The end effect is a unique taste experience that owes more to vintage oak-ageing that it does to the fact it is technically a beer.

Saison
Originally a summer beer style from Wallonie, the French-speaking south, it came in styles that varied from light and hoppy to sugary sweet. The best modern examples are a sub-style of what is becoming known as "farmhouse ale", a term that encompasses a range of blonde, amber and brown styles from the south.

NOTE: throughout this book the %age figures given for beer strength refer to their alcohol by volume

Stout

Local West Flanders' stouts tend to be low strength (4–5%) and sweet, in the manner of an old British milk stout like Mackeson, while in the rest of Belgium stouts are more often strong, dry and roasted, with some reaching barley wine strength and bursting with every flavour known to grace the world of beer.

Tripel

The Flemish Dutch word for triple, implying three times the malt/strength. Historically a dark brown strong ale style but nowadays usually a golden-blond, slightly sweet beer, again sometimes sanctioned by an abbey to raise money for the Order, though many lay ones exist too.

Wheat beer or White beer

Typically a lighter (4–5.5%) beer made with at least 30% wheat in the recipe. This causes a natural, hazy ("white") appearance. Most are flavoured with coriander, dried peel and other spices.

Trappist

An ale produced at one of the seven officially designated Authentic Trappist breweries. The beers are all brewed within an abbey under the auspices of the Trappist Order and all profits channeled into good works. Six of these are in Belgium. Trappist beer comes in all styles but the most typical is a strong brown ale.

Oak-Aged

A type of ale, usually though not invariably brown, associated mainly with West Flanders. Regular brown ale is set aside in oak casks for ageing for up to two years, at the end of which time it may be blended with fresh beer to make a sharp, mature, slightly sour, thirst quencher.

Typical British beers are roughly 3.5–4.5%, European and US lagers 5–5.5% and table wines 11–13.5%

Flemish café cuisine

There is a lot more to Flemish cooking than mussels and chips. Culinary excellence is a national obsession and its quality and diversity always impresses visitors. Most of the city's restaurants will describe their more elaborate dishes on English menus. Here are just a few of the commonly encountered bar meals.

Americaine – *cannibaal* (below) with a raw egg yolk.

Asperges – Belgian asparagus, most revered when it is white, monstrous and plumped up. The traditional Flemish way of serving is with chopped egg in melted butter.

Brochette – a proper kebab, featuring steak pieces skewered and char-grilled, typically with slices of onion and peppers.

Cannibaal – raw fillet of beef ground in mayonnaise with a little paprika, usually served on toast with raw carrot, gherkins, silverskin onions and Worcestershire sauce.

Carbonnade – beef, slowed cooked with a few vegetables in sour brown ale, with a little cream added.

Frites – the famous Belgian chips, lightly parboiled then twice fried. Belgians have stopped adding mayonnaise since the tourists started to do so.

Kikkerbillen – frogs' legs, usually of the small variety, acting mainly as an excuse for garlic and other sauces.

Mosselen – mussels, typically brought to the boil in a cooking pot with beer, celery, onion and herbs and served by the pot-load with *frites*.

Paling in 't groen – eel is particularly popular here near the coast and the most traditional preparation is cooked in a sauce of green herbs, typically chervil.

Pannekoeken – pancakes (Fr. *crêpes*), usually offered with a variety of sweet or savoury fillings.

Stoemp – mashed potato with carrot, leek or other vegetables in it, originally a Brussels speciality.

Stoofvlees – traditionally made from horse meat but nowadays usually beef, a thick meat and gravy stew that is slow-cooked for hours, sometimes in beer.

Uitsmijter – sliced cold ham on bread topped with three fried eggs, often served with mayonnaise and salad.

Vispannetje – mixed fish pieces in a creamy, sometimes cheesy sauce, cooked on a griddle in a cast iron pan.

Wafel – the Belgian waffle (Fr. *gauffre*).

Waterzooi – the traditional Ghent version of this creamy vegetable stew includes a whole chicken. Chicken pieces are more usual now. Coastal West Flanders has a fish version.

Witloof – white chicory, often served wrapped in ham and baked in a cheese sauce. The vegetable was first grown commercially in Belgium.

The various types of steak – *entrecôte, pave, Châteaubriand, filet* and others are presented with sauces such as *Bearnaise* (tarragon butter sauce), *archiduc* (mushroom), *Provençale* (Mediterranean vegetable), *Roquefort* (blue cheese) or *au poivre* (green peppercorn cream).

DUTCH–ENGLISH MENU TRANSLATOR

eend	duck
everzwijn	wild boar
forel	trout
garnalen	shrimps
haas	hare
haring	herring
heilbot	halibut
kabeljauw	cod
kip	chicken
konijn	rabbit
lamsvlees	lamb
Ostendaise	in a shrimp sauce
parelhoen	guinea fowl
patrijs	partridge
roomsaus	in a cream sauce
schol	plaice
staartvis	monkfish
tarbot	turbot
varken	pork
Vlaamse	Flemish
witloof	chicory
zalm	salmon
zeeduivel	monkfish
zeetong	Dover sole
zeewolf	sea bass

Bruges

1 @ **The Pub**
4 Hallestraat
T 0477 26 07 40
Open all week
Fri–Mon 17.00 to at least 03.00;
Tue–Thu 19.00 to at least 03.00
86 and building
Cheese and salami plates.

This new beer café opened in the late summer of 2008. It occupies a good spot in the centre of the city, to the right hand side of the Belfry looking from Markt, off Hallestraat to the right of the Witte Raaf restaurant.

It is a café of two rooms. The first is a small bar area with seating of the high stool perching variety, passed through on the way to the main lounge, which has bucket seats and mood lighting. There is an outside drinking terrace in a small courtyard for warmer weather.

A good place to hang out in for a beer into the wee hours, as many central bars close relatively early when the day trippers have gone and the overnight tourists are safely tucked up in bed. This bar stays open very late, even by Belgian standards, carrying on until daylight if trade allows.

What better to welcome the dawn than a big and beautiful **Abbaye des Rocs** (9%) from the brewery of the same name near the French border. This deep red ale is rich and fruity, and despite the brewery's absence of a real abbey, a homage to the great Belgian Trappist tradition.

2 2be 🏪 🍺
53 Wollestraat
T 050 61 12 22
www.2-be.biz
Open all week
🍷 **Shop** 09.00–19.00; **Bar** 11.00–19.00
🍸 200+
🍴 Belgian products to take away.

Most tourists will unwittingly have a photograph of this beer shop as it is housed in the impressive 15th century Mayor's house, viewed across the water from Rozenhoedkaai and the backdrop to one of the most snapped vistas in the city.

This is not obviously a shop, being down a covered hallway with no glass frontage to the street, a couple of doors down from Erasmus (below). Carry on down the hallway and you will find to the left a uniquely impressive 'wall of beer' display case of beers and matching glasses. The shop entrance is on the right, passing the huge flag logo to reach a warren of beautiful old rooms decorated in a pleasing modern style.

The theme is gourmet food and drinks that are 100% Belgian-made. There are biscuits, jams, marmalades, pâtés, pickles and a whole room dedicated to chocolate. We include it for the beers in the lower rooms, reached by staircases winding down to canal level. Roomy spaces are filled with huge shelves showing beautifully arranged displays of regional beers, matched to glasses. Even smaller Wallonian breweries get a look-in, unusual in Flanders. Is this the only beer shop in Belgium to have cushioned window seats to ease the strain of choosing the right purchase?

You can also sample beers on the highly photographed terrace, served from a few taps in a little bar to the rear.

Among the hundreds of beers available we feature a new one from an old brewery. The De Ryck family has been supplying excellent ales to the people of Herzele in East Flanders since 1886 through a network of small cafés. Recent expansion of their range has brought several new beers under the Arend ('Eagle') brand. **Arend Dubbel** (6.5%) is an exceptional beer for its strength with lots of dark rich fruit, caramel and malt flavours. A perfect beer for autumn.

Apero

3 Apero
11 Westmeers
T 0475 47 14 90
⊗ Shut Tuesday (except July and August)
🍷 10.00 til late
🍷 21
🍴 Bar meals, croques, pastas, omelettes.

Secreted in a corner of 't Zand, facing the massive Concertgebouw, Den Apero is a smart modern new café bar.

Bare brickwork and dark wood panelling are joined by a chandelier and clusters of those flock pattern lampshades that seem incapable of appearing alone, but rather gather in groups over bar counters, like thirsty posties at lunchtime.

The large screen TV often has the sound turned down, allowing the silent appreciation of sportsmen earning their living.

The beer of choice here is **Rochefort 8** (9.2%) from the Trappist abbey at Rochefort, in Namur province. To be allowed to be called an Authentic Trappist Product a beer must be brewed within the walls of a Trappist abbey, under the auspices of the monastic Order, with all profits going to the abbey and the worthy causes it supports.

Trappist beers come in a wide variety of styles but this green-topped classic is typical of the most prominent type, a dark brown ale. It pours opaque brown and is a smooth, roasted beer with fruity elements, much imitated, rarely bettered.

Atelier

④ Atelier 🍷 ✕ 🥪
8 Prinsenhof
T 050 44 78 88
www.kempinski-bruges.com
Open all week
🕐 10.30–01.00
🍸 13
🍽 Tapas, soups, salads, croques, nice nuts.

Found off Nordzandstraat, Kempinski Hotel Dukes' Palace is Bruges' first 5 star deluxe hotel. It was formerly the Prince's Court (Du: *Prinsenhof*), part of an estate built by Duke Philip the Good of Burgundy in 1429 where he founded the Order of the Golden Fleece to honour his wife and reward his loyal knights. Previous guests include Cardinal Wolsey, Thomas More, Erasmus and local Flemish master, Jan van Eyck.

The original Prinsenhof included a Ducal Palace, chapel, library, swimming pool, bath house, a hall for indoor ball games and a zoo. These are gone, though there remains a modern form of bath house in the guise of a spa, where you can pay to have hot rocks put on your back.

When it opened in Spring 2008, with 93 deluxe suites, each with a sitting room, we were delighted to find reasonably priced beer in its Bar Atelier at the back of the building, overlooking beautiful gardens in which are exhibited artworks from emerging talents. We liked the bright red poodles the size of houses.

The bar is modern, comfortable and littered with low tables and sofas to an artistic theme. The beers on offer are all from Palm brewery's much improving stable, including Brugge Tripel and Steenbrugge brands, Rodenbach Grand Cru in 75cl bottles and various lambics from the Boon brewery. From these we have chosen **Framboise Boon** (5%), the unfiltered, unsweetened raspberry lambic, produced by steeping raspberries and a few cherries in one- year-old lambic beer.

Most modern fruit beers are little more than glorified lager with added syrup but this is an authentic fruit lambic, with no artificial additives. Accessible enough for lambic virgins but not insulting to serious beer enthusiasts, it makes an excellent aperitif.

⑤ Bacchus Cornelius 🏪
17 Academiestraat
T 050 34 53 38
E info@bacchuscornelius.com
www.bacchuscornelius.com
⊗ Shut Sunday (Jan–Nov); **Tuesday** (all year)
◓ 10.00–18.30
🍸 400+
🍽 None.

You will often find tourists near this shop with their cameras pointing upwards towards the stone statue of the Bruges Bear, set in the Poortersloge building opposite. He is frequently dressed in weird and wonderful clothes, in the tradition of the Brussels' Mannekin Pis.

This is a great beer shop with a huge range from all over Belgium, including some sold nowhere else in the city. It is an excellent place to buy bottles to take home. Owner Inge is helpful and friendly. Beers include a good spread of lambics that have been fermented by natural, airborne yeast, a method of fermentation found uniquely in Belgium, mainly to the west of Brussels.

One such lambic beer on offer here is **Hanssens Artisanaal Oude Kriek** (6%) from Hanssens of Dworp, on the outskirts of Brussels. Most lambic brewers and blenders are carrying on a long-standing family tradition and Hanssens is no exception. Its roots are 19th century, the business having passed to the fourth generation, Sidy Hanssens and her husband John.

Hanssens do not brew their own lambic but rather buy it in from other brewers to store in oak barrels in the outhouses at the family's old farmstead. They then skilfully blend these beers to make gueuze or select individual barrels in which to steep cherries. These give this beer a fantastic sour, dry, fruit kick, which combined with the sparkle makes this a refreshing drink of some proportions.

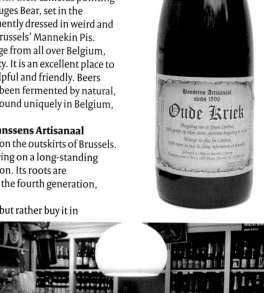

Bauhaus

6 Bauhaus

133–137 Langestraat

T 050 34 10 93

E info@bauhaus.be

www.bauhaus.be/restaurants

Open all week

08.00–02.00

41

Food (12.00–14.00; 18.00–23.00, 24.00 weekends). Good value and includes globally inspired pastas, pizzas, steaks and fish.

The Bauhaus is a budget hotel with a bar and restaurant, the latter recently rebadged as the Sacré Coeur, which has an online Dinner Dating Service from Sunday to Thursday, offering lonely Templars (m/f) an opportunity to dine with a partner found on their website. Sweet.

The bar has a nice traditional feel, still laid back but since a recent refurb no longer just aimed at young backpackers. All will feel comfy among the candelabras, heavy wooden beams, wax-dribbled candles and cream-washed bare brickwork. They still run an internet café with 15 terminals for those who need to contact home, or miss its computer comforts.

The Sacré Coeur has been revamped too and is more dimly lit than the bar, its deep red walls hung with ornate mirrors, medieval wall torches and antlers. It has a kind of contemporary Gothic feel. The huge unavoidable clock on the wall has a smaller brother in the other room.

Tall stools are arranged around the bars in both rooms, inviting you to settle down and order a beer. The selection of abbey beers is good, one of the best being **Maredsous Triple** (10%), brewed by the makers of Duvel. This is one of the biggest and strongest tripels in Belgium, a huge orange-blonde ale with a controlled sweetness balanced with fruity tastes and hoppy notes.

Belleman

❼ Belleman 🍷
22 Jozef Suveestraat
T 050 34 19 89
⊗ Shut Sunday & Monday
🕐 11.00–01.00
🍷 28
🍴 Light snacks, including pasta, omelettes and smoked salmon.

The tradition of the Belleman, or town crier, is as long-established in Belgium as in England. Indeed, the Flemish town of Ninove has hosted the annual World Town Crier Championship.

This street-corner bar is found on the way from Vismarkt to Astrid Park, one of inner Bruges' better kept secrets. This tranquil park and duck pond can be spared the milling crowds even in high summer, despite its children's play area.

This large corner bar is spookily English in style, with raised red velvet banquette seating and an aura of cosiness. They have collections of steins and banknotes and enough newspapers to keep abreast of world events, if your Dutch is good enough. Its owners are the Haacht brewery, Belgium's largest independent.

The sweet clear brown ale known as **Gildenbier** (7%) had its origins at the Cerckel brewery in the Brabantine town of Diest, north east of Brussels, where it was once typical of a local style, now long since passed. It has a deep amber colour, with less sweet caramel taste than it once had. Its brewers claim it pairs perfectly with chocolate. Well, you are in Belgium – go on!

⑧ Bier Tempel 🛒
7 Philipstockstraat
T 050 34 37 30
Open all week
🕐 10.00–19.00
🍷 600+
🍴 None.

Situated in a side road directly off Markt, the Beer Temple is an attractive beer shop which probably has the broadest range of Belgian beers under one roof in Bruges. It is also a good place to buy beer books, maps, gifts and paraphernalia.

The friendly staff can give expert advice about all aspects of Belgian brewing and know their stuff. If you are in Brussels, the owners have a sister shop of the same name in the Marché aux Herbes, opposite the Tourist Office, off Grand'Place.

They also have connections with the excellent café Cambrinus (below), further up the same street. Both offer a fantastic range of 75cl Wallonian beers, which can be difficult to find in Bruges.

Here however in the shop we feature something world class.

Podge Belgian Imperial Stout (10.5%) was originally brewed for a special tour group from Podge's Belgian Beer Tours www.podgebeer.co.uk, by the up and coming Alvinne Brewery in March 2005. After sampling four versions of the beer brewed with different yeasts, the tour group voted on their favourite version and this beer is what resulted.

As you might expect this is a big beer, black-brown with a good balance of sweet and dry. There are touches of chocolate, coffee, dark fruit, dates and roast malt too – something for everyone.

9 B-In

Oud Sint Jan complex
Zonnekemeers

T 050 31 13 00

E info@b-in.be

www.b-in.be

⊗ Shut Sunday & Monday

🕐 Tue–Thu 11.00–01.00; Fri & Sat 11.00–03.00

🍷 15

🍽 Full restaurant menu, from tapas to exotic European and Asian specialities.

In case you thought that Bruges' café society consisted entirely of ancient Flemish interiors with lace curtains and shelves cluttered with waffle irons, we thought we should lead you to B-In.

Although housed in the historic Oud Sint-Jan hospital complex this is a brilliant example of a café that achieves excellence through modern minimalist design, colour and exceptional use of light. Each of its three distinct spaces – restaurant, bar and lounge – has its own character. Bruges' flirtation with modernity does not always harmonise well with the old city but this one works.

You can either visit the restaurant to enjoy the city's most adventurous menu, conjured up by chefs who graduated from Belgium's top schools for the culinary arts, or just drop in for a beer on the terrace, or inside the bar area with its bare brick walls, excellent lighting and arty artwork. Friday and Saturday nights feature live DJ's.

Although the beer menu is on the short side it still manages to deliver a few crackers. On draught you will find **Brugge Tripel** (8.2%), a strong, sweet amber beer, with a fuller malt base than the average tripel. It used to be brewed in the now closed Gouden Boom brewery in Langestraat but nowadays comes from Palm, in the village of Steenhuffel in Flemish Brabant.

Bon Vivant

10 Dweersstraat

T 050 34 13 27

E lebistrobonvivant@hotmail.com
www.lebistrobonvivant.be

Shut Sunday

Mon–Wed 17.00-24.00;
Thu–Sat 12.00–13.45 & 17.00–24.00

10

Full restaurant menu, featuring charcoal grills from scampi and Dover sole to giant skewers of meat.

The Bon Vivant is found on a quiet street between the two bustling shopping streets that connect modern 't Zand square to ancient Markt.

Describing itself as a nocturnal bistro, as its name suggests it devotes itself mainly to food, specialising in dishes cooked on a charcoal range in the middle of the dining room. Local favourites include pork fillet or ham knuckle, each made with different sauces based on Tongerlo beers from Haacht brewery. They are also big on tourist menus that feature chicken.

Drinking without eating is allowed but with such a nice looking menu, you might change your mind and stay a while.

The beer menu is dominated by beers from Haacht, a stately looking large brewery situated near the town of the same name, between Leuven and Mechelen, in Flemish Brabant. One of the best is **Adler** (6.5%) a rare Belgian Dortmunder-style lager beer. It is golden-yellow in colour with a solid, white head and a grainy taste, like Pilsener with a heavier malt base.

Bottelier

11 Bottelier ⊗
63 Sint-Jakobsstraat
T 050 33 18 60
www.debottelier.com
⊗ Shut Sunday & Monday
🕐 Tue–Fri 11.45–14.00 & 18.45–21.45
🍷 1
🍴 Full restaurant meals.

A good five minutes walk off Markt, directly down Sint-Jakobsstraat, beyond Pietje Pek and Kleine Nachtmusik (below) is this real treat of a restaurant, offering food in a wide range of gourmet styles, fresh and seasonal, cooked to order. Their philosophy, 'Enjoy the time', refers both to the sourcing of food that is in season and to sitting back and relaxing in these beautiful surroundings. No rush.

The concept of time is underlined through the collection of timepieces on display throughout, including a group of little clocks cruelly trapped in a cage. You enter onto the middle of three split-level floors, each overlooking a lovely garden and canal. If you find yourself on the lower deck, take a look at the interesting photo montages reflecting times past, decade by decade.

Although there is an extensive wine list, there is only one great beer of note, but what a beer.

De Leite brewery at Ruddervoorde, near Bruges, is situated in a factory that makes designer shop fittings. It started brewing experimentally as long ago as 1988 but only went commercial with the launch of an amber-blond bombshell called **Femme Fatale** (6.5%) in 2007. It hits all the right taste notes being fruity, lightly spiced and with a good hoppy bitterness that pairs well with many dishes and is eminently drinkable.

⑫ **Bounce** 🍷
15 Burg
T 050 34 72 78
Open all week
🕚 11.00 til late
🍷 20
🍴 Croques, tapas, snacks.

opus Latino

Da Bounce can be accessed either from the De Garre alley, home to Garre and Cookie's (both below), or from the Galerij Ter Steeghere, which connects Burg and Wollestraat.

You need to like red to spend a lot of time here. The bar counter is faced with red light panels and the floor is black. The big feature here is the pair of red baize pool tables dominating the main room. They are very proud of their bingo machine, so we should mention that too.

Hidden away, this bar has a lovely, unexpected outdoor drinking terrace with a fine view straight up one of Bruges canals, towards Rozenhoedkaai, but this place really comes to life at night, when it mixes chilled and youthful. Sitting by the pool, so to speak, have a *waterpijp* (a.k.a. hubble bubble, hookah or shisha), a mere €10,00 for two coals and a beer.

If you are youthful and want to avoid tourists, this is the place for a late night **Rochefort 10** (11.3%), the ultimate floataway beer. Deep and delectable, this black-brown barley wine from the Trappist abbey of St. Rémy near Rochefort should be sipped and savoured. Ideal in such a night time haunt, it makes a great last beer (or two) of the evening.

Bretoen Pannenkoeken

⑬ Bretoen Pannenkoeken 🍷 ✗
4 Ezelstraat
T 050 34 54 25
✗ Shut Tuesday
🕙 11.30–20.00
🍷 18
🍴 Wide range of sweet and savoury pancakes.

This *crêperie*, or pancake house is a lovely one-roomed café in the homely style of a Breton kitchen, complete with red checked tablecloths.

Here they make sixty sorts of pancake, prepared, cooked and flambéed before your eyes on the large carousel griddle that dominates the café. The list of savoury pancakes includes ones stuffed with artichokes or coquilles St Jacques. The huge and tasty Popeye has spinach in a mornay sauce. Sweet *crêpes* include those flamed with Grand Marnier or Cointreau.

If you are all beered out, try the gorgeous Normandy cider in sweet or dry, served in a stoneware cup or if you are thirsty, in a half litre pitcher.

Beer drinkers are not forgotten though. Try the **Oerbier** (9%), the latest incarnation of the first ever beer from de Dolle Brouwers, a small independent West Flanders brewery that was in the

vanguard of the renaissance of Belgian beer brewing at the start of the 1980s. This reddish-brown beer is brewed using six different malts. It has a sharp, tart and distinctive taste. The logo "Nat en Straf" on the glasses means "wet and strong", a warning of its hidden potency.

Visit the brewery, three kilometres from Diksmuide, on Sunday afternoons. It remains at the forefront of quality and innovation.

⑭ Bron
82 Katelijnestraat
T 050 33 45 26
⊗ Shut Sunday & Monday and Feastdays
🕐 11.45–14.00
🍷 5
🍽 Full restaurant meals.

The Spring is a peaceful, cool haven of pale walls, tiled floors, cane chairs and white tablecloths, though you would never guess that from the somewhat forbidding brick and stone façade. With no menus outside to peek at you get no clue either that this is a lovely vegetarian restaurant and secret well of relaxed and healthy eating and drinking.

There is a main dining room and a lovely light conservatory-like space at the rear, behind iron-work lattice dividers. This tiny oasis is only open at lunchtimes, and not on Sunday or Monday. Apart from that what a little gem!

The beer list is tiny, but all grains used in the making of these beers enjoyed a good life roaming freely in the fields before being captured and turned into beer. This is because they are all organic, or what the Belgians call Bio.

Possibly Belgium's finest organic beers come from the great Brasserie Dupont in northern Hainaut. Four are available here, blonde Moinette Biologique, honeyed Bière de Miel Biologique, wheat beer Blanche du Hainaut Biologique and the lightest, **Biolégère** (3.5%).

The low gravity of Biolégère makes it excellent for lunchtime drinking. It also shows that good Belgian breweries can brew great tasting beers of low alcohol too. Biolégère is a classic of the saison style that was brewed with quite high hop levels in late spring for consumption by agricultural workers in the fields in summer. Delicately spicy from the yeast used, with a nice underlying bitterness, this is a world class light ale.

Brugs Beertje

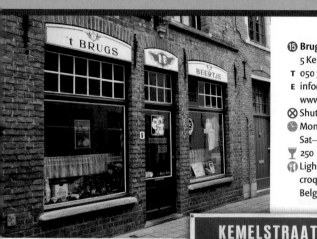

15 Brugs Beertje 🍷
 5 Kemelstraat
T 050 33 96 16
E info@brugsbeertje.be
 www.brugsbeertje.be
⊗ Shut Wednesday
🕐 Mon–Tue & Thu–Fri 16.00–01.00;
 Sat–Sun 16.00–02.00
🍷 250
🍴 Light snacks, including spaghetti bolognese, croques, cheese, pate and salami plates and a five Belgian cheese plate with bread and side salad.

KEMELSTRAAT
oude huisnaam

Well where do you start?

The Little Bruges Bear is an unassuming place just off Steenstraat, a street of shops joining 't Zand to Markt, opposite Simon Stevinplein. Since opening in 1983 it has gained worldwide fame, becoming an international beer lovers' shrine but remaining a place also for locals. On any night of the year you will find it packed with beer drinkers of all ages and nations.

So why does this ordinary looking brown café make it onto every Grand Beer Tour of Europe? Without question it has a special atmosphere all of its own that many bars have sought to copy but none has matched.

This is a particularly good bar to visit if you are out on your own. Perch on a bar stool and you will soon find yourself in conversation with someone who may come from Copenhagen, Vermont, Grimsby or a couple of hundred metres down the way. Beer is the universal language.

Owner Daisy Claeys and her staff are supremely knowledgeable about the Belgian beer world and expert at helping out bewildered patrons. Even when busy, which it often is, service is excellent and always friendly. It is unsurprising that many people who travel to Bruges only ever visit this one bar, such is its quiet

perfection. The huge beer menu is arranged by region and brewery. The beer list rotates its draught beers (always five, never a Pils) and is always up to date with new breweries and new beers from old breweries, often with a seasonal theme.

The café has always had a special relationship with local brewer Johan Brandt, who started his Regenboog brewery in an old smithy in Assebroek on the outskirts of Bruges in 1996. It recently moved to a village near Oudenaarde in East Flanders and changed its name to Smisje but the local loyalties remain.

Many of Johan's beers are all but unavailable in Belgium as most goes for export, mainly to the United States. But you can usually find them here. Famed for experimenting with unusual ingredients, in the past he has used mustard in his beer Wostyntje, sloes in Sleedornbier and pumpkin in Halloween. A bee keeper in his spare time, Johan also brews with honey.

Honey joins dates in the recipe of **Smisje Dubbel** (9%), strong dark ale in the dubbel style. As with all brews from Smisje, the style is given a twist, differing from other dubbels in part through its strength (though it does not drink like a 9% brew) and in part its taste. It pours cloudy dark amber rather than the traditional brown and tastes sweet, with caramel, and dark fruit notes but a little sourness in there too for balance.

Be sure to warm it up to room temperature to appreciate its complex sweet, cakey aroma and flavours.

27

Cafedraal

⑯ Cafedraal 🍷 ❌
   38 Zilverstraat
T 050 34 08 45
   www.cafedraal.be
❌ Shut Sunday
🕐 12.00–15.00 & 18.00–23.00
🍷 6
🍴 Fish, shellfish, meat, game.

Although it is in the centre of Bruges, this bar is easily missed. It can be entered either from Zilverstraat or via the courtyard-shopping square, Zilverpand. The latter entrance takes you through the lovely garden and terrace, which looks incredible at night when changing globes of coloured light glow among the olive trees.

The building dates from the 15th century, which is not that unusual in Bruges. What is unusual is the brilliant renovation, with one eye to the medieval and the other to quirky modern. By day the place is noticeable for its high ceilings, dark wood and church-like interior. By night it is brought to life by clever use of light effects.

The entrance hallway is adorned with real hams, suspended from the ceiling, complete with little paper cuffs to catch the dripping fat...Mmmm. These are set off by ham-shaped ceiling lights that just about illuminate the gloom, supplemented by paper lights in the shape of fish, or they might just be real dried fish with light bulbs.

Behind the bar is a riot of classic candelabras and contemporary neon. It works. The interesting light effects extend to the toilets. Every wall, floor and ceiling surface is a glass panel, which gradually changes colour, whilst you are seated. Marvellous, entertaining and disconcerting in equal measure.

Other rooms in the building are given over to a restaurant where comprehensive food menus rule, in contrast to a stumpy little beer menu.

At least they stock **Duvel** (8.5%), the top-selling strong golden ale from Duvel Moortgat of Antwerp province. This is a rare example of a high production ale that remains of high quality, though an all-important expansion at the brewery in the near future will test the company's brewing skills and political resolve.

In its distinctive glass this straw-coloured spritzy ale is deceptively innocent.

Cambrinus

⑰ Cambrinus 🍷 ✕
19 Philipstockstraat
T 050 33 23 28
www.cambrinus.eu
Open all week
🕘 11.00 til late
🍺 400
🍴 Bar snacks and full meals,
including some cooking with beer.

Although the building in which it is housed dates from 1699, its latest incarnation as a café-restaurant only opened in 2006.

Just off Markt, its name is a corruption of Jan Primus, or John the First, one of the early Dukes of Brabant, whose appreciation of the finer things in life extended to banqueting and excellent ale.

The design is English pub style, with dark panelled walls and brass lights. It was created by the same people who converted Dickie's (below) and the Botteltje café of the Hotel Marion in Ostend, though the hand-painted wall decorations are more recent.

Although you can dine heartily here, they also serve snacks and nibbles. There is a children's menu too.

The beer list is as daunting as it is brave. Most of the 400 brews are described in a huge bound volume encased in wood covers. Written in three languages, it tries openly to tempt Pils drinkers into trying something less dull.

Unusually for Bruges it stocks quite a few 75cl bottles, an ideal way for sharing a beer with two or three friends, being sure to pour it all in a continuous flow, leaving the sediment in the last centimetre or two.

Among these is **La Rulles Estivale** (5.2%) from the Rulles brewery in the Pays de Gaume, perhaps the best of many excellent new breweries in Luxembourg province. First brewed to celebrate the fifth anniversary of the brewery, this light, golden refreshing hoppy beer is brewed for the spring season, but can be enjoyed throughout the year.

Capucientje

18 Capucientje

72 Westmeers

T 050 33 92 04

E guido.monstrey@telenet.be

www.capucientje.be

⊗ Shut Monday; Wednesday (Nov–Mar)

🕑 Tue & Sun 11.00–20.00; Thu 11.00–18.00; others 11.00–22.00

🍺 40

🍴 Bar meals, including frogs' legs, omelettes and scampi.

On one of the routes between the railway station to 't Zand square, you will find the Little Capucine café with a great umbrella-covered courtyard terrace that is open from March to November. You can also access it via a little path over the bridge from King Albert Park.

This is one of Bruges' many 'Tea-rooms', a quaintly English term for a sort of up-market café that serves drinks, light meals, ice cream and freshly made pancakes, waffles or whatever. It is not unusual for these to have a significant beer list, as is the case here.

Beers from Sint-Bernard, Bosteels and the Reinaert range from Proef brewery are joined by **Gouden Carolus Classic** (8.5%).

This is one of the beers brewed by the recently revitalised het Anker brewery in Mechelen, between Brussels and Antwerp. Essentially the subject of a management buy-out a decade ago it has gradually gone from strength to strength, including opening Belgium's first brewery hotel on site.

The city of Mechelen was always famed for its brown ales and this one maintains that tradition. A big, beefy, dark ruby red ale, it has the warm, soothing qualities of an old classic, nudging towards greatness.

⑲ Celtic Ireland
8 Burg
T 050 34 45 02
E brugge@celticireland.be
www.celticirelandbruges.be
Open all week
11.00 til late
21
Bar meals, including lamb stew
and Irish haddock.

Belgium likes its Irish bars, but does not usually plonk them in the middle of its most historic squares.

The menu states that the interior design is based on the Book of Kells, presumably in its Flemish edition. This bar is all dark red walls, Celtic knots and megaliths. The claim that, "the beautifully carved wooden bar back will leave a lasting memory", is not far off the mark. The area around it is usually the most lively, but this is a huge place with several quieter rooms and a massive dining area upstairs.

There is live music every night, which sometimes has to compete with the TV when there are big sporting events.

Surprisingly for an 'Oirish bar' they do great food. Lamb stew is the Hibernian staple, steaks and battered haddock less so. We assume the spiced monkfish tail in coconut and a 'Celtic' sandwich featuring Cajun chicken on foccacia bread are hang-ons from the days of the Irish Empire.

You can find Guinness and Kilkenny on draught, but for an unusual Belgian, go for **Bourgogne des Flandres** (5%), literally Flemish Burgundy, from Timmermans brewery, near Brussels. This dark red beer imitates the Flemish old brown style using a lambic base, tasting sweet, sour and hugely fruity. It is on draught here, which is a rarity.

They have a huge selection of whiskies too. Slainte!

Cookie's

20 Cookie's 🍺 ✖
   2 De Garre, *off Breidelstraat*
T 050 61 35 88
   www.cookiescafe.be
✖ Shut Wednesday
🕐 Mon, Tue, Thu 18.00 til late; Fri–Sun 16.00 til late
🍷 20
🍽 Tapas, hot, cold and grilled on the big grill
   from 18.00.

This ancient building from 1600 is another down the tiny blind alley De Garre, off the short cobbled way that joins Markt and Burg. Its original purpose was as an ancient fire escape from the backs of buildings in this part of medieval Bruges.

This particular building was once an ingredients store of well-known Bruges biscuit maker Edward Corneille, though it is more directly named in honour of its current owners the Koekelbergh-Grenelle's who bought the place at the end of 2006.

The bar area is dominated by a large open grill that springs into life at 18.00, when it is put into use grilling various tapas. The kitchen has a Spanish–Italian–Flemish theme, which means a wide range of tapas dishes hot and cold on top of the grills.

This tiny bar has a lovely upper floor with a balconied area looking past the huge light fitting formed by a frame of tea lights on a rope pulley down to the ground floor beneath.

Fittingly, you can drink **Cookie Beer** (8%) from the Ecaussinnes brewery in northern Hainaut. This is a blonde beer with added flavouring of a type used in the particular Belgian biscuit known as *speculoos*, which often accompanies a coffee. The spices featured are ginger and cinnamon, which add to its sweetness. A dessert beer, perhaps.

21 Coolcat
11a Eiermarkt
E coolcatbrugge@telenet.be
www.dominicus.be/coolcat/info.html
Open all week
12.00 til late
17
Bar meals, snacks, croques, spaghetti Bolognese, finger food.

Bruges' centre for nightlife of the sort enjoyed by excitable youth (and older tourists who are all-historied-out) is Eiermarkt, the old egg market.

This modern bar, like the rest on the square, comes to life at night, when the music is Belgian dance/trance, with all that it entails.

Its tiny entrance gives way to a tardis-like space inside and a long bar that snakes its way back to a window onto Niklaas Desparsstraat beyond. The front is bar stool seating only, but there are tables further back, and on the outside terrace at the front.

Like a sour old gueuze will cut its way through heavy Flemish grandmother cooking, so the Coolcat can razor through the excesses of a weekend full of Gothic architecture, Flemish masters, fabulous dining and light Baroque string quartets.

It is a sign of the increasing awareness of beer among young Belgians that in the sort of place that a couple of years ago would stick with Stella and worse, there are three Chimays and a Dubuisson on the beer menu.

This last is **Cuvée des Trolls** (7%), the kid brother to Dubuisson's extraordinary range of strong ales, sold as Bush in much of Europe and Scaldis elsewhere. Unfiltered, with a tendency to be cloudy, this blonde ale uses dried orange peel to impart a fruity, sweet flavour.

Curiosa

22 Curiosa 🍷 ✖
22 Vlamingstraat
T 050 34 23 34
E info@curiosa-brugge.com
www.curiosa-brugge.com
✖ Shut Monday & Tuesday
🕐 Wed–Fri 11.30–15.00 & 18.00–23.00;
Sat 11.30–24.00; Sun 12.00–22.00
🍷 37
🍴 Full restaurant menu, steaks, fish,
mussels, salads, omelettes.

Vlamingstraat runs off Markt. After a hundred metres or so, look out for the street sign for this 16th century cellar bar, which is entered down some very steep stone steps.

Its two rooms each have beautiful vaulted ceilings. Religious icons make for interesting décor. If you are lucky you might get the seat next to an odd figure of Joseph holding the baby Jesus, whose face has, rather disconcertingly, fallen off.

Although steak and *frites* is the obvious favourite here there is a more adventurous restaurant menu, such as the ostrich steaks, eel, lobster, and a nod to beer cuisine in the rack of lamb with wheat beer and Flemish stew made with Brugse Zot Dubbel.

Verhaeghe brewery at Vichte near Kortrijk is one of West Flanders' undersung heroes. The fourth generation of Verhaeghes continue to brew and age the traditional versions of Flemish brown ale, which is kept in oak tuns for up to two years before blending and bottling. This was one of the first small breweries to make a large investment in new and refurbished oak vessels.

Their flagship beer is the deep reddish brown **Duchesse de Bourgogne** (6.2%) and this can be found at the Curiosa. The lovely oaky taste comes from fermentation rather than absorbing anything from the wood. Its slightly sour but deliciously mature character can shock initially but usually wins people over.

Flemish Art of Brewing

DUCHESSE DE BOURGOGNE
Br. Verhaeghe Vichte

Dell'Arte 🍷 ✕
28 Vlamingstraat
T 050 34 20 64
E francois.feytongs@skynet.be
http://dellarte.michelangelo.be/en/home.htm
✕ Shut Thursday & Friday
🍷 Sun 11.00–22.00; others from 09.30 til late
🍷 18
🍴 Full restaurant menu, including
filet mignon, traditional lamb stew
and a good selection of fish.

The café Dell'Arte is a comfortable tea-room
and restaurant, situated opposite the
Bruges opera house.

There is a bit of a Fifties/Sixties retro
theme, with old film posters dotted about.

Service is fast and attentive.

On the way to the toilets you pass
through a room filled with a scary amount
of Elvis memorabilia.

Mechanical features in the toilet do
everything except the paperwork.

Food starts with breakfasts, progresses
to great lunches, to pancakes and waffles
in mid-afternoon and then on to dinner.
The menu changes with the seasons and
can be interestingly gamey.

The suggested beer is Brigand,
from the Van Honsebrouck brewery at
Ingelmunster, near Kortrijk. This comes
served with a dish of fresh radishes.

Brigand (9%) used to be a ginger-
coloured amber beer but went blond a
year or two back. It is a solid, strong
blond ale that drinks its weight and can
get you in a mood to have a second.

24 Dickie's 🍷 ✖
16 Vrijdagmarkt
T 050 52 03 11
E dickiesbeerandgrill@hotmail.com
⊗ Shut Wednesday
🕐 Mon–Fri 11.30 til late; Sat 09.30 til late;
Sun 15.00 til late
🍷 80+
🍴 Full restaurant menu, including
Côte à l'Os and king prawns in garlic.

How many pubs do you know that are named after the dog? Dickie is the dachshund – the one found shuffling round the bar as if he owns the place.

His beer and grill house can be found on that corner of 't Zand that leads to Smedenpoort, next to the place where coaches from all over Europe drop and pick up their day-trippers. If you are one, make this your first and/or last stop.

During the week grills tend to be an evening thing (to 22.00) though they run all day at the weekend (to 23.00). During the day in the week there are lighter snacks, apple pie and home-made ice-cream.

There are usually a couple of special beers on draught, plus a clever list of bottled brews, which grows around Christmas time. The list features many of Belgium's better breweries such as Kerkom, from near St Truiden in Limburg, 3 Fonteinen of Payottenland, and an exceptional newcomer, Alvinne, from near the Kortrijk ring road in Heule.

Alvinne Extra Restyled (7%) is a more heavily hopped light amber version of the beer that preceded it and is one of the new additions to the portfolio of a brewery that is clearly and obviously growing in confidence and competence. This marks their first use of American hops in a beer, which bring with them a gloriously intense citrus bitterness with a dry finish.

㉕ Druid's Cellar 🍷
11B St Amandsstraat
T 050 61 41 44
www.youtube.com/watch?v=ncIGf5ztsDQ
⊗ Shut Monday
🕐 Tue–Sun 11.00 til late
🍷 20
🍴 Pastas, spaghetti bolognese, lasagne, toasties, Sunday lunches.

All you expect from an Irish bar and a little bit more.

A stone's throw from Markt, but hidden underneath the Lange Muur (or Great Wall) Chinese restaurant, this candlelit cosy cellar bar is dark by night and day, but warm in its welcome.

They are a sporty bunch and have a dartboard in the front bar and a huge pool table in the big back room. Televisions showing UK football are in both front and back bars and are popular for the big games. There is a pub quiz every Sunday at 21.00 and live music every Thursday from 21.30.

Irish and Scottish whiskies of course are in abundance, but when in Belgium, beer is the drink of choice.

The short beer menu includes Druïde Blonde brewed at the Proef brewery but we have selected the signature beer of Wallonian Brabant's Lefèbvre brewery, **Barbār** (8%).

Named not after the elephant, but an abbreviation for the barbarian depicted on its label. This pale blond ale is brewed with a light form of honey in the mash. The first hit is alcohol, followed by some of the subtler honey flavours. Manages to be sweet without being cloying.

26 Dyver ✕
5 Dijver
T 050 33 60 69
www.dyver.be
⊗ Shut Wednesday & Thursday afternoon
🕐 Mon, Tue, Fri & Sat 12.00–14.00;
others 18.30–21.00
🍸 1 on tap, plus others to match food.
🍴 Full restaurant menu, including
cooking with beer.

It was 1992 when Guido Vandenbussche and his late wife Lies moved the focus of their attention from De Garre (above) to their dream of a restaurant serving food made with beer as an ingredient paired with a glass of beer matched to each course.

Named after the canal it borders, Den Dyver is one of the restaurants that has led the development of fine Belgian beer cuisine and in 2007 was rewarded with the gold medal in Belgium's Beer & Gastronomy Awards.

The dining experience is in the grand style, and both the setting and the service reflect this. This is not the place to roll in off the street after a day long pub crawl to be loud over a nice plate of something and a few more bevies. Rather savour the experience and expect fine cuisine in measured portions from a highly refined menu, accompanied by a small measure of an appropriate beer.

The menu will always feature something interesting enough to tempt the most jaded palate. Imaginative use is made of fresh local seasonal produce. Each dish is cooked with a specific beer, and you tend to be served with this beer to drink with it. This invariably comes with information, related by your waiter, about the beer, who brews it and why it is used in the dish you have chosen.

To the frustration of some and the relief of many, there is no beer menu. This is dictatorial drinking and as they have been doing it for so long we respectfully suggest that you go with the flow.

It is wise to make a reservation, as its quality has made it very popular indeed.

To start your gastronomic experience we recommend a glass of the house beer, a slightly aged version of **Augustijn** (8%), a blond tripel beer from Van Steenberge of Ertvelde, north of Ghent, which is for some reason always better here.

27 Erasmus 🍷 ✕ 🖂
35 Wollestraat
T 050 33 57 81
E info@hotelerasmus.com
www.hotelerasmus.com
⊗ Shut Thursday
🕐 12.00–23.00
🍷 125
🍴 Full restaurant menu, including
a wide variety of classic and
new-style Flemish cuisine.

We do not like being pushy but a visit here is compulsory.

The owner of the Erasmus, Tom Allewaerts, has been promoting Belgian beer with quiet enthusiasm for over 30 years, in which time he has taken this café, restaurant and hotel through many phases to being a much-loved place for beer enthusiasts from around the world.

Tom has been so successful in creating his restaurant that it now has a Michelin star, so those lazy evenings with a few old Brugean punters have given way to exquisite dining accompanied by superb beers, but less room for drinkers.

If you just want a beer it is best to come in the afternoons or at quieter times out of season, when you can watch the horse carriages and poor oblivious tourists pass by while sitting in a stylish and peaceful café, with classical music, great beer and no sense of rush.

Upstairs the ancient-and-modern bedrooms offer a comfortable treat with the guarantee of a great buffet breakfast.

The beer selection is hard to beat, for its ten draught beers with their seasonal bias – Easter beers at Easter, Christmas beers at Christmas and so on – plus limited edition beers.

Although you can find a huge selection of beers in Bruges those from the Slaghmuylder family brewery in Ninove, west of Brussels, are under-represented. One of their best brews is **Witkap Stimulo** (6%), a refreshing, light straw blond ale with a sharp citrus tang that is especially fine as an aperitif.

Estaminet

28 Estaminet 🍷
5 Park
☎ 050 33 09 16
⊗ Shut Monday
🕐 Thu 16.00 til late; others from 11.30 til late
🍷 32
🍽 Pastas, snacks, croques and sandwiches.

There is no British translation of the French word Estaminet, though Establishment shares the same derivation and 'village pub' gets the drift.

This one abuts Astrid Park. In the summer there is a terrace at the front to soak up the sun and it is heated for cooler evenings. While the outside is bright and airy, the café itself is of the brown café or *kroeg* variety, Belgian shorthand for an older, cosy, worn-in beer haunt.

Food is wholesome and good value, especially the pastas.

Every town has its dependable late night boozers, and often the best of these will have a jazz and blues theme. This one comes to life in the evening, when the jazz and blues soundtrack mixes with the animated conversation of locals. Can it afford to be anything other than dimly lit, with bags of charm?

They keep offerings from De Struise Brouwers, or Sturdy Brewers, a unique bunch of innovative brewers who are having great fun pepping up the Belgian beer revival with some very special and tasty beers made at Deca brewery not far from Ieper (Ypres). One of their top beers is the dark and brooding **Pannepøt** (10%), classified as a strong brown abbey-style beer termed 'quadrupel' by Dutch and American importers but with a nod to a traditional Flemish oak-aged styles.

㉙ Ezeltje 🍺
 118 Ezelstraat
T 050 33 25 74
 Open all week
🕐 Mon–Fri 12.00–14.30 & 18.00–02.00;
 Sat & Sun; 16.00–02.00
🍷 24
🍴 Spaghetti bolognese, croques,
 cheese croquettes, shrimp croquettes.

The Ezeltje, or for fans of legendary Austrian singing duo Nina & Frederick "Little Donkey", is a small, one-roomed locals' bar situated just inside the ring road on the way to the suburb of Sint Pieters.

It is a cosy, long narrow room with small tables, though most locals here seem to congregate around the bar on high stools. They can be seen playing the famous *mort subite* dice game at the bar. Ask nicely and the owner will explain the rules.

There is a small outside terrace at the rear which can be sat in during the summer months. In winter you can watch it on the CCTV behind the bar.

Here the lost art of putting your tab on a very sharp nail driven into a piece of wood thankfully survives despite European Health & Safety legislation.

The donkey theme extends to the beer list and features three donkey-related beers. The Bassevelds Ezelsbier is a dry blond from Van Steenberge. The café also offers the blond wheat and the brown Ezel beers from Bavik Brewery, in Bavikhove, south of Bruges. **Ezel Bruin** (6.5%) pours more amber than brown and is a good, solid malty drinking beer.

30 Fiore
15 Hauwerstraat
T 0478 52 36 91
⊗ Shut Wednesday & Sunday
Mon, Tue, Thu 10.30–20.00; Fri 10.30 til late;
Sa 08.00 til late
15
Light snacks.

This is a place where *Kitsch* has been allowed to go mad.

Owner Patricia has made her bar a shrine to all things tasteless. It is only a small one roomed café, but how much is packed into that room?

Much of the ornamentation, as its name suggests, is on a flower theme. There are beautifully clashing garish pink and orange walls with gaudy flowered rose wallpaper. These same walls are adorned with naff 60s and 70s LP covers that look like knitting patterns for camp men. There are flowery plastic table cloths in livid colours, vases with plastic roses, canary bird cages with plastic goldfish, gnomes, gooey-eyed fawns, knitted wool ornaments and a lot of coat hangers.

On the beer front, Patricia thankfully ditches her sense of humour and stocks **Westmalle Dubbel** and **Triple**. To make her happy, order a 75cl bottle of **La Chouffe** (8%) and share it.

A perusal at the label will tell you why she selected this beer. Gnomes, apparently, are not allowed at Chelsea Flower Show as they are considered tasteless tat. But they feel at home here.

La Chouffe comes from the hamlet of Achouffe in the Luxembourg Ardennes. Until recently it was an independent brewery but in 2006 was bought out by Duvel Moortgat. Pundits feared the worst but they have put a lot of investment in and thus far at least taken none of the quality out. Production has increased and this easy-drinking, strong, coriander-infused blond ale has both kept its character and increased its reliability.

31 Ganzespel 🎭 ❌ 🍽
37 Ganzestraat
T 050 33 12 33
E nicky.s.B.B@skynet.be
www.ganzespel.be
❌ Shut Monday & Tuesday
🍷 12.00–14.00 & 18.30–22.00
🍷 22
🍲 Full restaurant menu, including local specialities and daily specials.

This tiny café restaurant is just around the corner from the Nieuw Museum (below) and thus a wee bit off the beaten track.

The Goose Game is a traditional board game set out in the form of a snail, a bit like snakes and ladders, but without the snakes. Or the ladders. If you want to know more, look to the walls where there are examples.

The step-gabled house also accommodates Nicky's Bed & Breakfast with three rooms above and the restaurant and bar below. The restaurant consists of a small number of candlelit tables, which makes dining an intimate experience. Its menu is strong on local dishes and steaks, with an additional daily menu that offers exceptionally good value.

The owners are fond of Trappist beers, which feature prominently on the beer list. Most Trappist breweries are represented. Chimay is probably the best known of Belgium's Trappist breweries, their beers being brewed within the abbey at Scourmont in southern Hainaut, under the auspices of the Order.

You will find their beers on many menus throughout the city, usually in 33cl squat bottles. Here however, they serve the larger corked 75cl bottles, going under the name **Chimay Grande Réserve** (9%). Although this is the same beer as the smaller Chimay Bleue, the larger bottle seems to assist in the development of flavour, giving a bit more depth and a rounded character to this big, strong, brown beer which has hints of roast malt and caramel.

Garre ✗ ✗✗✗✗

32 Garre
1 De Garre, *off Breidelstraat*
T 050 34 10 29
⊗ Open all week. Shut last weeks of January & June
🕐 Sat 11.00–01.00; others 12.00–24.00
🍷 130
🥪 Sandwiches.

The business card here reads, "De must in Brugge" and it certainly is. To find it, look out for the tiny alley from which it took its name, off to the right on Breidelstraat as you walk from Markt towards Burg, the two big squares in the city centre.

The small downstairs room is the epitome of Brugean elegance. A tiny staircase leads to an equally small balcony room upstairs. To be served a beer you need to be seated, which can be difficult at weekends.

A long-standing favourite of beer lovers round the globe, it has a huge beer list (with no Pils!). This alone makes it memorable but there is something in the atmosphere that makes this the café that more that any other is the one people remember with nostalgia. ("Do you known the one down that alley?")

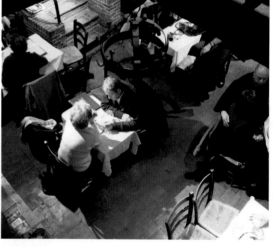

Your chosen beer is lovingly served on a mini tray with a doily, and a tiny dish of cheese. Enjoy this to a background of gentle Mozart. This bar is famous for playing Ravel's Bolero as the last tune of the evening, which signals "Time, gentlemen please!"

Amongst the many fine beers here is **XX Bitter** (6.2%) from de Ranke brewery of Dottignies near Mouscron in northwestern Hainaut. It is renowned for its massive hop presence but unlike some of the super-hopped herbal medicines found in California and elsewhere, flavours of citric and floral hoppiness dominate. Deploying a top quality malt recipe adds good balance, making this a classic beer.

⑨ Gezelleke 🍺 ❌
15 Carmersstraat
T 050 33 83 81
www.chouffeclub.be
❌ Shut Saturdays & Feast days
🕐 Mon–Thu 11.00–24.00; Fri 11.00 til late;
Sun 10.30–14.00
🍷 22
🍴 Bar snacks including goat's cheese croques
and *vispannetje*. Kitchen open until 23.00.

The Gezelleke café could translate into
English as the "Cosy Little" though it
also makes allusions to the Flemish
poet and proponent of the language,
Guido Gezelle, who lived round here.
    You will find this self-styled 'eating
and chatting' place on the road that links the centre to the
windmills on the ring road, in what might be termed mews
Bruges. This pretty, old-style Flemish café with high ceilings
and a black-and-white tiled floor has a single candlelit bar.
    Two beers vie here to be the house specials.
    La Chouffe is one, as the owners are friends of
Kris Bauweraerts who founded the original brewery in
Luxembourg province, deep in the Ardennes. Kegs of this
beer go on sale on the third Friday of every month at 21.30
when regular Achouffe evenings are celebrated.
    The second contender is **Guido** (8%), not only for the
Gezelle connections but also because is comes from the
former Regenboog brewery on the outskirts of Bruges,
now Smisje of Mater-Oudenaarde. We plumped for the
second as Smisje beers are well worth sniffing out.
    The beer is a hazy orangey brown with a sweet,
fruity and spicy taste, brewed with honey and raisins.

Goldies

34 **Goldies** 🍷 ✕
  18a Kerkstraat (Damme)
T 050 67 30 04
E info@goldies.be
  www.goldies.be
⊗ Shut Tuesday & Thursday
🕚 11.30 til late
🍷 33
🍴 Bar snacks including pasta, sandwiches and desserts.

Goldies is a newly refurbished modern café right on the corner of the Markt in Damme. The name is a condensation of Golden Oldies and the bar follows this theme with picture discs of earlier decades adorning the walls.

There are two separate bar rooms inside and a sizable drinking terrace out, with a great view of the square and the statue of Jacob van Maerlant. He is seen as one of the great Flemish poets of the Middle Ages and lived in Damme in the 13th century.

As well as the famous Trappist beers, made under the control of real monks, Belgian brewers make a number of abbey beers that have been approved by the national brewers' organisation because they are made by agreement with various religious orders and organisations that benefit financially from their production. There are about seventy such beers.

Ramée Blonde (8%) is one of these. It is an unusual beer to find in Damme, being made for Jacques Mortelmans, who has led the restoration of the spectacular buildings of Ramée abbey near Jodoigne, in Wallonian Brabant. Until recently it was brewed close to the French border in western Hainaut by the Brunehaut brewery, but is now brewed at du Bocq brewery in the Meuse valley north of Dinant in Namur province.

The beer is golden, bitter and slightly on the tart side.

Gran Kaffee de Passage

35 Gran Kaffee de Passage 🍷 ✕ 🗕
26–28 Dweersstraat
T 050 34 02 32
E info@passagebruges.com
www.passagebruges.com
✕ Open all week. Shut mid-Jan to mid-Feb
🕑 Fri–Sun 19.00–01.00; others 19.00–24.00
🍷 27
🍴 Full restaurant menu, including
some cooking with beer and a
good vegetarian choice.

Dweersstraat links Noordzandstraat and Zuidzandstraat, off 't Zand, where you will find this hotel, hostel, café and restaurant business trying hard to offer best value and high quality in all its many lines of work.

The main bar is decorated in the Art Deco *fin de siècle* grand café style. There are sumptuous cushions on the bench seating, where you can eat and sip your beer while staring at the giant stags' heads at the far end of the bar, or at the huge heater in the centre of the room which resembles part of a steam engine.

Meals here are in what the Belgians call the Burgundian tradition, from the days when the Dukes of Burgundy ran the northern branch of the Hapsburg Empire from various bases in what was then called the Low Countries.

The beer menu is marked up on huge wall mirrors and includes several beers from the Sint-Bernard brewery, set among the hop bines west of Poperinge, near the French border. One of these is the huge and incredible **St. Bernardus Abt 12** (10.5%). The brewery describes this beer as "the show piece of the brewery". Few would disagree. Definitely one to have with a meal – why not go for the full-on Burgundian blow-out.

This hefty-sounding beer has a dark mahogany-hued glow, and an alluring aroma. Its warming brandy richness is offset by great deep fruity flavours, and it is wonderfully smooth. Am I the only one licking my lips?

36 Gruuthuse Hof ⊗
36 Mariastraat
T 050 33 06 14
E Gruuthusehof@gruuthusehof.be
www.gruuthusehof.be
⊗ Shut Wednesday & Thursday
🕙 10.00–21.00
🍷 14
🍽 Full restaurant menu,
including excellent fish.

Set on the corner of Heilige-Geeststraat (Holy Ghost Street) and Mariastraat in the shadow of the Onze-Lieve-Vrouwekerk (Our Lady's Church) this café is in one of the most photographed zones in Bruges. It has been run by three generations of the same family since 1955.

The restaurant name refers to the grand house across the road (now a museum) which in the late Middle Ages belonged to the family of the lords of the Gruuthuse. These merchants held a monopoly over the sale of *gruut*, which was a medieval mix of herbs and spices needed in the brewing of beer as a flavouring and preservative. They were the oil barons of their day.

The big draw here is the classical Flemish cuisine, with their forte being fish dishes in all their simplicity and complexity. Expect to find creations based on all the Belgian coastal favourites such as sole (*zeetong*), trout (*forel*), monkfish (*zeeduivel*), mussels (*mosselen*), salmon (*zalm*) and the excellent tiny North Sea grey shrimps (*garnalen*). There are meat and chicken dishes too.

The beer featured in Gruuthuse Hof is however *gruut*-less.

Petrus Oud Bruin (5.5%) is brewed 50 km south of Bruges at Bavikhove by the de Brabandere family's Bavik brewery. This is a blend of regular brown ale and a beer which has been aged for two years in oak tuns. As a result, Oud Bruin has a dark red hue, a vinous, slightly sourish character and is a perfect thirst quencher.

37 Halve Maan 🍺
26 Walplein
T 050 33 26 97
E info@halvemaan.be
www.halvemaan.be
Open all week
🕐 10.00–18.00
🍷 2
🍽 Bar meals.

The smell of brewing is back in Bruges once more.

Prior to the 1914–18 War the city centre could boast more than thirty active brewhouses. By 2004 there were none. When the Half Moon brewery on Walplein ceased brewing their famous Straffe Hendrik beers it was because the company that owned the brand, a bigger brewery at Dentergem, did not think the brewery still owned by the Vanneste family, descendents of founder Henri Maes, were up to it.

This so miffed them that when the parent company restructured in 2005 son Xavier, newly graduated from brewing school, fired up the plant to produce a new beer, **Brugse Zot Blond** (6%). This has been joined by a dubbel, a Dutch-style bok in autumn and most recently the return of Straffe Hendrik in its original 9% version.

The name means 'Bruges's Fool', from a remark by Hapsburg Emperor Maximiliaan, who visited the city in the 15th century amidst wild festivities. On being asked for funds to build a new lunatic asylum he suggested that putting a roof over the city might suffice.

You can sit in the former bottling hall and enjoy a beer or a tasty meal from a menu that includes cooking with beer. If you want to find out more about the history of the brewery join one of the 45-minute tours that leave on the hour every hour from 11.00 to 15.00 (16.00 in summer) and followed with a tasting of the unfiltered Brugse Zot Blond on draught, sold only here at the brewery.

You can find the filtered version at almost every café in the city nowadays. This is such an easy-drinking, likeable blond brew that even a lager drinker should be able to understand it.

Hof van Rembrandt

38 Hof van Rembrandt 🍷
   10 Eiermarkt
T 050 33 74 50
   www.thofvanrembrant.be
   Open all week
🕐 11.00 til late
🍸 35
🍴 Snacks including pasta dishes, omelettes and salads.

The Rembrandt's Court in Eiermarkt, a small square off the main Markt, is surrounded by cafés, many of which are targeted at younger drinkers from home and abroad and which often stay open into the early hours. This one is more middle-aged, surviving nicely without the need for flashing lights and dance music.

In summer its trade comes from its large umbrella-covered sun terrace, while in winter the bar has an open fire for cosy night-time huddling.

They are keen here on Trappist beers, to the extent that they dominate the beer menu. As well as supporting the Belgian Brothers they also import a couple from over the border in the Netherlands, offering beers from the only non-Belgian Trappist brewery, at the abbey of Koningshoeven near the Dutch city of Tilburg.

These beers take the brand name 'La Trappe' and the Rembrandt has both the Tripel and the mighty **La Trappe Quadrupel** (10%). This strong ale pours a coppery-amber colour and tastes surprisingly crisp and fruity for a beer of this weight. Strength of this magnitude brings an almost inevitable sweetness, in this case offset by the detectable hop presence. One to be respected and slowly savoured.

⑨ **Hollandse Vismijn** ⚲
　4 Vismarkt
T 050 33 33 01
⊗ Shut Tuesday
🕒 08.00 til late
🍷 27
🍴 None.

Holland is strictly that part of the western Netherlands that stretches from north of the Schelde delta to the old Zuiderzee inlet, now the Ijsselmeer lake. Whether it has any fish mines is open to question.

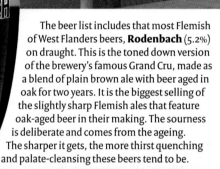

This unforced café looks out onto Bruges' open air fish market, a stone built colonnaded affair that dates back to 1821. A small selection of fresh North Sea delights is laid out on the stone slabs every morning from 08.00 to 13.00, barring Sunday. With complete disinterest in international tourism, the camera-tolerating fishmongers ply their trade almost entirely in Flemish Dutch, avoiding any indulgence in the myriad languages usually heard elsewhere. Sales are mainly to locals, who feel this is still their part of town.

Despite its local allegiances, the café welcomes all, allowing a brief escape from tourist prices too.

The bar expresses political leanings in its décor, with a red rose stained glass panel and photographs of local politicians. Beats horse brasses.

There is a heated terrace for those who like to be toasted on chill winter evenings. As elsewhere this morphs into a sun terrace in warmer months.

The beer list includes that most Flemish of West Flanders beers, **Rodenbach** (5.2%) on draught. This is the toned down version of the brewery's famous Grand Cru, made as a blend of plain brown ale with beer aged in oak for two years. It is the biggest selling of the slightly sharp Flemish ales that feature oak-aged beer in their making. The sourness is deliberate and comes from the ageing. The sharper it gets, the more thirst quenching and palate-cleansing these beers tend to be.

Jerry's Cigar Bar

⑩ **Jerry's Cigar Bar** 🍷 🖩
13 Simon Stevinplein
T 050 33 77 94
E info@jerrycigarbar.com
www.jerrycigarbar.com
⊗ Shut Sunday
🕐 08.00–19.00
🍷 12
🎵 None.

Don't tell them in California, New York, Ireland or the UK but some countries actually have bars that encourage people to smoke.

Jerry's Cigar Bar is in the corner of Simon Stevinplein square, halfway along Steenstraat between 't Zand and Markt, opposite the side street that is home to Brugs Beertje (above).

Jerry's is an incredibly well-stocked cigar shop with stoggies from all over the world and a cosy modern bar attached at the rear. The place is well worth a visit even if you don't smoke cigars, but a welcome retreat for those who do so with great pleasure.

The range displayed in humidors around the shop is enough to make you want to think of taking up the noxious weed as a new obsession. Watching Americans worry about whether they should try the Cubans is a hoot. Yes, but don't inhale, Brad?

The menu offers a Balmoral cigar and a drink of the week, or a coffee cognac matched with its own cigar or best of all, a **Tripel Karmeliet** (8%) with a Cohiba.

The bar stocks other beers from the Bosteels brewery of Buggenhout, northwest of Brussels but we feature Tripel Karmeliet, a strong blond ale that it is brewed using three grains – unmalted wheat, malted oats and malted barley. The result is a really characterful, sweeter than average but superb tripel the construction of which can even appeal to those who generally prefer drier beers.

Kelk 🍷

69 Langestraat
T 0473 73 34 60
www.dekelk.be
Open all week
🕐 17.00 til late
🍷 +/-195 and building
🍴 *Crôques.*

Ah! The Chalice.

This dark, candlelit, laid-back place is normally awash with Champagne paraphernalia but looks as if things are about to change. The walls are set to come down and new rooms are being opened up at the rear of these sprawling premises. There is even talk of a beer shop upstairs.

Although it is aimed at younger drinkers, old farts are welcome, if only because they can often remember the words to the background music better for having been there when it first came out.

No such problem for Zucchero the Dalmatian because he is deaf and will lounge lumpenly at your feet and sniff. He can (and does) bark loudly but he is friendly.

The beer list is being expanded along with the building. The menu is little more than a rough guide, as new beers come and go all the time. Ask what is new, though even the baseline list is impressive, with a range of more than thirty abbey beers and plenty of smaller breweries represented. This includes a good spread of lambics. In the winter season watch out for the huge range of seasonal beers.

There is a move towards beer education too, with tastings once in a while.

It is hard to pick one beer from such a great menu, but why not go for the rarely found and excellent **Vicaris Generaal** (8.8%), a beer brewed for Dilewyns of Grembergen by the Proef brewery. This is a dark brown, luscious beer with a taste so complex it has been likened to the iconic Westvleteren beers. It tastes hoppy, chocolate-cakey, spicy and dark fruits are in there somewhere.

Kleine Nachtmuziek

42 **Kleine Nachtmuziek** 🍷
60 Sint Jakobsstraat
T 050 33 50 84
⊗ Shut Wednesday
🕐 18.00 til late
🍷 43
🍴 Light snacks –
pastas and salads
in summer.

This cosy, relaxed café has a Sydney Greenstreet fan and two pianos as room dividers. There is much Guinness and whisky memorabilia along with candlelight and friendly service. Despite the name, its music selection leans more towards blues, folk and rock than Mozart.

The menu comes in a lever arch file and features huge quantities of whiskies from Scotland, Ireland and the USA. The beer menu is not massive but this is a quality list, featuring the complete range of beers from the Roman brewery near the East Flanders town of Oudenaarde, including their Ename Blond and Dubbel on draught. You can also find ultra-hoppy XX Bitter and Guldenberg from De Ranke and the lovely Saison Dupont and Moinette Blonde from Dupont brewery.

Although many styles of beer are found in Belgium, strong stout is a relative rarity. One brewery produces a corker, though. **Hercule Stout** (9%) is one of Belgium's premier stouts and comes in a distinctive stoppered bottle. It has a gorgeous burnt coffee, chocolate and liquorice flavour.

The beer has been brewed at the Ellezelloise brewery, next to an old farm overlooking Ellezelles in northern Hainaut, said to be the birthplace of Agatha Christie's fictional detective Hercule Poirot, after whom the beer is named. The brewery was recently merged with another micro, the Géants brewery of Ath, to form the Brasserie des Légendes. Whether this will lead to changes in the beer, who knows?

Kluiver

43 Kluiver

12 Hoogstraat

T 050 33 89 27
E hendrik@dekluiver.be
www.dekluiver.be

Shut Tuesday & Wednesday

Sat & Sun 11.00 til late; Mon & Fri 16.00 til late; Thu 18.00 til late;

Full meals, changing menus featuring steaks, fish and snacks.

A *kluiver* is the Dutch name for a particular sail, found on some of the sailboats that ran the routes from the North Sea to Bruges before the Polders silted up. This is the theme for this small cosy bistro-bar, just off Burg. Consequently the ceiling is dressed in billowing canvas and there is a serious collection of biscuit tins and tea caddies on the walls featuring sailing boats of every kind.

The beer we feature here is the Belgian Trappist classic, Orval, from the abbey of Orval near Florenville in one of the most attractive parts of the Ardennes, in Luxembourg province.

The design on the bottle is derived from the legend of Mathilda of Tuscany, who visited the site where the original abbey was being constructed in 1076. On putting her hands into a nearby spring, the wedding ring given to her by her late husband slipped off and fell into the lake.

After praying for its return, a trout is said to have appeared on the surface of the water with the ring in its mouth. And they all lived happily ever after.

Whatever you think of the story, **Orval** (6.2%) is certainly a legendary beer. Orangey-amber in colour, it has a peppery, hoppy bitterness and a long dry finish that comes from being brewed with a slow-acting *Brettanomyces* yeast culture. It gets better when aged in the cellar for a year or more.

Krakele

44 Krakele
63 St. Pieterskaai
T 050 31 56 43
www.dekrakele.be
Open all week
07.30–24.00
30
Bar meals, full meals, snacks, tea room.

Found on the ring road, a 15 minute walk from the city centre, the Krakele is a huge modern roadside café with a prominent outside drinking terrace. It is also a hotel, banqueting hall and tea-room all rolled into one. It takes its name from the nearby bridge.

You can order full meals such as Flemish stew or lasagne, or go for waffles, pancakes and ice-cream (probably not all three).

The current building dates from 1971, though there are some nice old black and white photographs of the previous structure on the site, which was a well-known farm and dairy that used to sell milk direct to the public. Amazingly, the business is still in the same family but instead of milk, they will serve you a beer.

The choice of ales includes sound staples from regional brewers, such as Van Eecke, but a rarer find is the deeply traditional **Ichtegem's Oud Bruin** (5%) from Strubbe brewery at Ichtegem, founded in 1830, the same year as the state of Belgium. This is another Flemish brown ale in the style that blends young sweet beer with older aged beer to give a refreshing drinking experience.

45 Kuppe
19 Kuipersstraat
T 050 33 39 20
www.dekuppe.be
Open all week
Sun 14.00 til late; others 11.00 til late
100
None.

This hard-working, beery café is found just behind the Opera House, not far off Markt.

Seating on stools at the bar is popular with locals and you can smoke here as they do not serve food. By day this is a pleasant and quietish place to call in for a couple of beers. By night they crank up the music, people start drifting in and it springs to life, continuing well into the night.

If it gets too busy and you cannot get to the loos, there is always the handy stainless steel pissoir opposite, in full view of a number of cafés and restaurants.

The Kuppe has a wide choice of quality beers at some of the best prices in town. Highlights are several beers from Van Den Bossche, de Dolle Brouwers, Sint-Bernard, Dubuisson, Roman and Bavik, plus Rodenbach Grand Cru.

The beer menu is generally light on lambics, though they feature one of the very best – **3 Fonteinen Oude Geuze** (6%). This is produced by Armand Debelder at his 3 Fonteinen brewery in Beersel. Sometimes equalled, rarely bettered, Armand has been at the heart of the fight for survival of this incredible group of beer styles. Against all the odds, in a world filled with commercially produced sweet beers, authenticity is finally winning through.

Lambic beer is unique to Brussels and the Payottenland area to its West. After being fermented by wild yeast from the atmosphere, it is matured in oak casks for up to three years. To make gueuze, younger sweeter lambic is expertly blended with older, sourer, flat lambic up to three years of age. The result is impossible, absurd and quite unlike any other form of drink you will ever encounter.

Finest dry cider meets extract of aged burgundy against a vaguely grainy backdrop. If you have not tried lambic beers before, suspend everything you have learnt about beer thus far and approach this more as if it is a barrel-aged drink that is officially beer but in reality something unique.

Expect to be shocked by your first but to get it just enough to be tempted back for a second.

Lamme Goedzak

46 Lamme Goedzak 🍷
31 Noorweegse Kaai
T 050 28 86 10 (Damme Tourism)
www.bootdammebrugge.be
⊗ Shut October to March
🕐 From Bruges 10.00, 12.00, 14.00, 16.00 &
18.00; from Damme 09.15, 11.00, 13.00,
15.00 & 17.20
🍺 13
🍴 Crisps.

One of the more novel places to drink quality beer is on board the good ship Lamme Goedzak, which spends half the year ploughing backwards and forwards along the four kilometres of canal between Bruges and its former port of Damme.

Known as the Napoleon canal, this long straight stretch of water was built in 1810 by Spanish prisoners of war on the orders of Napoleon Bonaparte.

The pick up point at the Bruges end is just outside the ring road beyond Dampoort. Get there from Markt or 't Zand by the number 43 bus and if you miss the boat, the bus will take you on to Damme itself.

The boat makes its way more sedately and completes the pleasant journey in just over half an hour. Single fare costs €5,50, return €7. Naturally the boat has a bar on board, so you can while away the journey with a beer in hand.

Most of the beers are from the country's oldest family brewery, Roman, founded in 1515, which boasts some twelfth generation family members on its Board.

The Roman beer we feature is their **Ename Dubbel** (6.5%), an abbey beer in the dubbel style. It is light bodied with plenty of sweetness and a caramel follow-through.

47 Lamme Goedzak
13 Markt (Damme)
T 050 35 20 03
www.lammegoedzak.be
Shut Thursday
11.00–21.00 (in July closes at 22.00)
<10
Full restaurant meals.

Pretty both outside and in, this is a classic Flemish restaurant, in a prime position opposite the elegant, bijou town hall, in which busy nesting swifts dart backwards and forwards high above the bus stop back to Bruges.

The Lamme Goedzak restaurant has been here since 1952 and is the oldest continuously running in Damme. Prior to this, the building housed the village school.

Inside is a comfortably elegant downstairs room with a galleried upper floor from which you can stare down on the taxidermy and the diners below. There is an enormous stone fireplace, which must have made the erstwhile school the warmest place in town.

For summer open-air dining it has a beautiful garden terrace at the rear set round a central fountain and tables out front on the square. The place took its name from one of the characters of a book by Flemish author Charles De Coster, who the author had 'born' in Damme.

Lamme Goedzak (7%) is also the name of a beer from Scheldebrouwerij, which continues to have its offices in the Netherlands but in 2008 moved its brewery over the Belgian border to Meer in northern Antwerp province. The beer started life one degree lighter but the restaurant owner here

wanted a stronger beer and persuaded them to pep it up.

This is a very full bodied, dark golden brew with an effective bitter-sweet balance of hops and malt which make it a fine, tasty beer in the Belgian strong pale ale style.

Leopold

48 Leopold
26 't Zand
T 050 33 19 87
E alain.talloen@pandora.be
⊗ Shut Wednesday & Thursday
🍷 10.00 til late
🍷 36
🍴 Spaghettis, pastas, croques, omelettes, pancakes.

The modern kingdom of Belgium was created at the London Conference of 1830. Its first king, Leopold I, fought at Waterloo and was first married to the daughter of the English King George IV, who would have ascended the British throne had she not died after a miscarriage in 1821.

During his 35-year reign Leopold created a country that developed so rapidly and confidently that its progress continued despite the reign of his son, Leopold II, the only monarch of recent times to take a country (Congo) as his personal fiefdom.

Anyway, this family-run bar with its splendid view of the new concert hall, is a shrine to all things Leopold. Owner Alain Talloen is proud of his impressive collection of enamel signs featuring the beers and breweries that Belgium has named after its favourite King, some over 70 years old.

As well as offering substantial snacks, there are lots of cakes, ice-creams and pancakes for the 't Zand Square afternoon tea crowd.

The beer menu is a model of clarity with a picture of each bottle and glass alongside tasting notes and the strength of each beer.

Alain recently added to his beer list Van Steenberge's **Gulden Draak** (10.5%). The beer is named after the golden dragon (copper in real life) that perches atop the clock tower in the city centre of Ghent. Legend has it that the original was so beautiful that it caused wars between the medieval power brokers of Ghent and Bruges. Ghent got the dragon, but you can still drink the beer in Bruges.

This big, powerful beer certainly drinks its weight. Apart from the alcoholic moreish sweetness there is a good body which it makes an excellent sipping beer.

49 Lokkedize 🍷 ✕
  33 Korte Vulderstraat
T 050 33 44 50
E letsgobruges@skynet.be
  www.lokkedize.be
✕ Shut Monday & Tuesday
🌙 18.00 til late
🍺 18
🍽 Full restaurant menu, including Greek
  cuisine till 24.00, 01.00 Fri & Sat.

"Hard to find – worth the discovery"
say the owners, referring to the fact
that this is only one block the wrong
side of 't Zand, off Zuidzandstraat.

If you are tiring of Flemish master chefs,
come here for good standard Greek cooking with
plenty of retsina, tsatsiki, feta salad, taramaslata
and calamari on the menu. The service is fast
and friendly and the atmosphere is convivial.

Its attractive candlelit interior has exposed
brick walls on which musical instruments
are displayed. Although there is quality
food here, it is enough of a café to stay open
unusually late and expect customers whose
main interest is late beers. There is live
music on the last Sunday in the month.

Our featured beer here is the world-famous
Westmalle Tripel (9.5%) brewed at the
Trappist abbey in the north of the country.
This beer is available in many otherwise
unbeery Belgian cafés, often a godsend among
the standard wares of the global brewers.

In 1956 this was the original blond tripel.
Before then tripel meant a dark beer. It is
amber-blond with a powerful, smooth taste
that can be enjoyed in the day but is more suited
to late evening drinking. This is the tripel
against which all other brewers measure the
inadequacy of their own. Be wary of its strength.
Remember you have to live tomorrow also.

Marieke Van Brugghe

50 Marieke Van Brugghe
17 Mariastraat
T 050 34 33 66
www.mvb.be

⊗ Open all week. Shut all of January
Sat & Sun 10.30–22.00; others 10.30–21.30
10
Full restaurant meals. Seasonal dishes and Flemish stew made with Kasteelbier.

Everyone agrees that Bruges looks great. Yet for all its quiet pomp, the only two pieces of important history in the place are found in seen-better-days Onze Lieve Vrouwekerk (Church of Our Lady) opposite this great institution. Inside is Michelangelo's Madonna and Child, the only work to leave Italy during his lifetime and a substantial influence on Flemish artists of the day.

In the crypt is the mausoleum of Duke Charles the Bold of Burgundy and his daughter Mary, whose marriage into the Hapsburg dynasty began the definition of what we now take as the design and style of modern Europe.

'Little Mary of Bruges', with its prominent outdoor terrace and elegant dining indoors is not as classically quaint as you might expect on this historic corner. Rather the design is contemporary, with pale wooden cladding on the walls, rising to barrel-like rolls towards the ceiling where an interesting light fitting of counter-weights and mirrors sits over a design that makes clear reference to Michelangelo.

The food is top notch and the prices not as daunting as the efficient looking, black and white waiters would suggest. We suspect the nearness of the church explains the sweets in the shape of the Blessed Virgin that are served with your coffee. On Sundays in particular, it just does not feel right biting her head off whilst she is praying. But when in Rome, as they say.

This is the first place in Bruges to serve **Kasteel Triple** (11%) on draught. You might want to try it with a big dessert, since sweet is this beer's hallmark. An uncompromising brew from Van Honsebrouck, it is golden in colour and drinks like a barley wine, leaving a warm after burn like spirituous liquor.

Meridian 3 🍺 ✖
15 Markt
T 050 33 50 32
www.meridian3.be
Open all week
🕐 08.00–23.00
🍷 15
🍴 Breakfasts, steaks, fish, club sandwiches
and incorporates an ice cream parlour
(Opens at 08.00 for breakfast.
Kitchen open 11.00–23.00).

This recently opened modern tea room and ice cream parlour has outstanding views across the famous Markt from its terrace and ground floor, but even better ones from its upper floors.

The building is interesting, even by Brugean standards, being the oldest on the square, with a conspicuous golden spiked ball on its roof.

It could easily be mistaken for a decorative architectural folly but the menu gives an explanation, in English. Quetelet's ball is made of copper and was installed in 1837, being the last remaining in Belgium. Adolphe Quetelet was appointed in 1836 to map meridian lines in 41 Belgian cities in order to standardize for the first time the measurement of time. This in turn was made necessary by the arrival of new-fangled railways to Belgium in the previous year.

The meridian line of 3 degrees and 11 minutes east of Greenwich runs through the building, hence the ball on the roof and the name of the café. A row of brass plates in

the square mark the line and in days gone by noon was determined when the shade of the ball fell on the brass plates and the town hall clock was adjusted accordingly.

The great view in summer makes this a pleasant place to drink Palm Brewery's new wheat beer, **Steenbrugge Wit** (5%), which is light and refreshing with just a hint of spice.

Nieuw Museum

52 Nieuw Museum 🍺 ✕
  42 Hooistraat
T 050 33 12 80
  www.nieuwmuseum.be
✕ Shut Saturday afternoon & Wednesday eveni
🕙 11.00—14.00 & 18.00 til late
🍷 40
🍴 Full meals, including steaks and seafood
  grilled over the open fire and snacks.

A short walk out along the canals away from the city centre will bring you to this great little grill house and old-fashioned café. The traditional interior has a quarry tiled floor, a huge map of old Bruges, various quaint knick-knacks and a festoon of hop bines.

Many of the people who come here have been drawn by the spectacular grills, cooked over the huge open range in the middle of the bar. The main room is dominated by the sights, sounds and smells of the grill with the coming and going of meat and fish being cooked and plated up.

If you had not come to eat, you may change your mind when the charcoal is in full swing.

Great food and beer have combined in this superb family-run establishment to make a new room necessary to accommodate the overflow.

The beers here come from all across Belgium, with a good representation of Trappists and an ever-changing *wisseltap*, or guest draught beer on the fifth tap. One of the stars on the menu is the world classic **Saison Dupont** (6.5%).

The first thing you notice on opening this golden ale is its distinct flowery aroma. Next comes a billowing hop presence that dominates through aromas and herbal flavour, but not an unbearable bitterness. It is the most accomplished of the modern versions of the *saison* style of beer from Wallonia. There farmhouse ales developed differently in different localities but in the modern era, this is the one against which all others are judged.

Nieuwe Tempelier

Nieuwe Tempelier
120 Gistelsesteenweg
T 0497 46 86 92
Shut Sunday & Monday
Sat 10.00 til late; others 16.00 til late
16
None.

Travel is a human game; discovery is its prize.

To discover the Nieuwe Tempelier you need to travel out of town from the corner of 't Zand down Smedenstraat, under the railway tracks and at the junction keep to Gistelsesteenweg. It should take no more that ten minutes on foot and is less than five from the Parazzar (below), on parallel Tourhoutsesteenweg.

Entering from the street you will see nothing more unnerving than a good local pub, with perhaps an above-average interest in pub games such as pool, table football and pinball. But ask for the arrows and they will not hand you the darts. Instead you get sent out back, where you will find a fully kitted out archery lane. And if that does not suit, it can convert into a Flemish-style bowling alley.

This is a real community pub, or *lokaal*, would you believe, untainted by tourism. In Belgium, these are often meeting places for local clubs and this one happens to be the HQ of an archery club, cycling club, darts club, football club, country dancing group and the local philatelists. Lots of Cercle Brugge fanmobilia on display too.

People tend to gather round the bar in this Bavik house. The beer menu features most of the brews from family-owned Bavik brewery, including four on draught. Their **Pilaarbijter Blond** (7.2%) is a relative newcomer to the scene and a beer of quality. It is a golden blond, spicy brew.

The unusual label features a man biting a pillar, taken from Pieter Breugel's painting "The Flemish Proverbs." In Dutch a 'Pillar Biter' is a hypocrite.

54 On The Rocks
5 Grauwwerkersstraat
T 0 50 33 20 37
www.ontherockscafe.be
⊗ Shut Monday
🕐 Tue–Sun 19.00–05.00
🍷 24
🍽 Bar meals from omelettes to Ribeye.

The business card says "drinks, tapas and music go together". We'll dance to that.

This is another place that looks unpromising from the outside, especially when closed, but is well worth investigating as a late night drinking bar.

This is a dark tunnel of a café, its long, narrow main room opening into a square seating area at the rear. Its superb high wooden drinking bar and leaning shelf is reflected in the mirrored wall opposite in the dim light.
Retro high tables and stools abound, all upholstered in a post-modern orange and brown moquette. Pink neon lights behind the bar complete the look.

The un-mirrored parts of the walls are decorated with Tony Bennett and Petula Clark album sleeves from the Seventies, a nod to subversive interior design rather than a reflection of the music policy, though we did get a Dutch version of Cole Porter's *I Love Paris* followed by Desmond Dekker's *Israelites*, an Irish jig and Dusty Springfield's *Son of A Preacher Man* one after another, so they do eclectic.

Here you will find another beer list favouring Trappists, with the usual suspects from Chimay, Rochefort, Westmalle and Orval. This extends to relative novitiates at the St. Benedictus cloister at Achel.

Achelse Kluis Trappist Achel Bruin (8%) first made an appearance in 2001 and has been improving ever since. Though it lacks the heavy presence of Westmalle Dubbel it has a drinkability more associated with a regular brown ale, plus hints of candy sugar and chocolate.

55 **Opkikkertje**
13 West Gistelhof
⊗ Shut Sunday
🕐 Mon,Tue,Thu,Fri 16.30 til late,
   Wed 18.00 til late, Sat 17.00 til late
🍷 25
🍴 None.

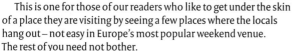

You do not have to get far out of town to find quiet residential streets in inner Bruges. The name of this local bar, which seems to be particularly popular with postmen, translates roughly as "Pick-me-Up". Hopefully not appropriate as most park their bikes outside.

This is one for those of our readers who like to get under the skin of a place they are visiting by seeing a few places where the locals hang out – not easy in Europe's most popular weekend venue. The rest of you need not bother.

A basic, locals bar rather than Baroque-tapestry-lace Bruges. There is a front room with a type of table football, lots of stools that migrate to the bar to be perched on by customers, and large barrels that double as tables.

The beer selection is above average for a small locals bar but there is no beer menu to choose from. Instead, judge what is on by the display of bottles on a shelf by the bar.

These change from time to time but a permanent fixture is **Kapittel Abt** (10%) from Van Eecke, a sort of blond tripel only bigger. The top of the range and weighing heftily it nonetheless cleverly manages a certain subtlety of flavour, though alcohol dominates.

56 Origin'O Brugge – De Trog 🏪
142 Katelijnestraat
T 050 33 31 37
www.origino.be
⊗ Shut Sunday
🕐 Mon–Fri 08.30–18.00, Sat 08.30–17.00
🍷 <10
🍴 Take away organic food and snacks.

The principle of the small Origin'O chain of food and drink shops is that they specialise in fresh and organic products, including beers. De Trog means 'the Trough', so go on, make a pig of yourself.

Amongst the shelves of fresh daily deliveries of fruit and vegetables, freshly baked breads and cakes, cheeses and Breton seaweed you will find nestled some unusual beers including an organic range from Dupont – Moinette Biologique, Bière de Miel and Saison Dupont Bio, plus Lousberg from Proef brewery.

They also sell another organic beer from Proef, called **Gageleer** (7%). This golden ale is made with bog-myrtle from a marshy part of the Kempen in eastern Antwerp. Myrtle has been used in beer making for centuries and is said to have been one of the principal ingredients of *gruut*, the much valued herbal mixtures used in making beer in the Middle Ages.

The recipe for this beer originated with a Kempen home brewer and revives the tradition of using this shrub in brewing.

Gageleer tastes characteristically of myrtle, which is a bit like pepper and eucalyptus, but it is also spicy and refreshing.

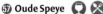

57 Oude Speye
7 Kerkstraat (Damme)
T 0476 40 97 94
Shut Wednesday & Thursday
12.00–22.00
20
Full restaurant meals.

On the corner of the main village square of Damme, a short walk from the moorings of the Lamme Goedzak (above). Parts of the building date from the 13th century though it has only been a cafe for four hundred years or so.

Outside the front of the café there is a small drinking terrace on the cobbles. Inside is a large, square, high-ceilinged room with a traditional yet modern interior, with dark brown furniture and walls, offset by a nice cream painted wooden ceiling, joists on display.

Nowadays this former beer café is more of a restaurant, though you can still just pop in for a beer.

One surprising find on draught is **Floreffe Prima Melior** (8%) from the Lefèbvre brewery in Wallonian Brabant.

This is an abbey beer, made under licence granted by the Abbey of Floreffe, the name of which comes from the Latin for flower. Founded in 1121 and itself housing a brewery from the 13th to 18th centuries, it was closed when the abbeys were abandoned after the French Revolution.

Prima Melior means literally 'the best'. It is a dark brown beer flavoured with aniseed and coriander. Anyone old enough to remember Spangles will get it straight away.

Oxfam Wereldwinkel

58 Oxfam Wereldwinkel 🛒
8 Geldmuntstraat
T 050 33 11 68
E brugge@oww.be
www.oww.be
⊗ Shut Sunday
Sat 10.00–18.00; others 09.00–12.30 & 13.30–18.00
🍷 2
For self-catering only.

Oxfam shops in Belgium are different from British ones. Instead of selling second hand clothes they go by the title of World Shop, because they specialize in selling new products sourced from individuals and small groups around the world. They concentrate on Fair Trade and organic produce.

This shop is to be found on the less populated of the two shopping streets that link 't Zand and Markt. Items on offer include small household goods, clothes, toys and jewellery.

They also sell food and drink products such as rice, spices, teas, coffees, wine, and two specially brewed bottled beers.

These both come from the Huyghe brewery at Melle, near Ghent and contain quinoa from Bolivia, basmati rice from India and cane sugar from Costa Rica. Quinoa (pronounced 'keen-wa') is a high protein super-seed that is being promoted for its lack of gluten, high nutritional status and, well, export potential. It has a light, delicate taste and is used in the mash for **Oxfam Bruin** (7.5%).

Oxfam Bruin has a dark mahogany colour and an interesting complex, sweet taste.

59 Pallieterke 🍷 ✕

28 't Zand

T 050 34 01 77

E pallieterke1@telenet.be

www.pallieterke.com

⊗ Shut Monday & Tuesday

🕐 11.30–21.30

🍷 17

🍽 Full restaurant menu, including
rabbit with prunes, mussels,
fish *waterzooi*, beef carbonade.

The name of this café comes from a novel by Flemish author Felix Timmermans, which depicts the joyousness of rural Flemish life around the character of a happy-go-lucky consumer of waffles and of beers called Pallieter.

Like most of the establishments on or near 't Zand, this one has a restaurant at the back of an all-year-round front-facing conservatory, appropriately heated in the winter.

We include it not because it is different from the rest but rather because it is plainly among the very best, with a well-prepared and adventurous menu, and friendly, efficient service.

Full meals are available throughout opening hours and those ubiquitous waffles, pancakes and ice creams can be ordered between 14.00 and 18.00, should you be feeling peckish.

The café stocks several beers from the Sint-Bernard brewery in the heart of the hop fields of West Flanders. These include **St. Bernardus Prior 8** (8%) a dark chestnut ale in the dubbel style, a little on the sweet side but fulsome with a lace of pear drops.

Panier d'Or

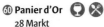

60 Panier d'Or 🍷 ❌
28 Markt
T 050 34 32 34
www.restaurant-tompouce.be/
panierdor/nl/index.php
Open all week
🕐 09.00–23.00
🍴 5
🍴 Full restaurant menu, with lobster
the speciality of the house.

The Golden Basket sits in an unbroken row of cafés on one side of the old square, facing the Belfry. It might just be the most photographed café in Europe, having appeared on holiday snaps, tourist brochures and the cover of beer books ever since the invention of the camera.

Like all cafés on Markt, it is quite expensive, but its great view of the leaning Belfry tower, particularly splendid when lit up at night, is worth a bit extra.

Incidentally, the climb up the tower is 366 steps to a panoramic take on the city and in fine weather a view to the coast 12 km away. You can also see the clock mechanism close up, and if you are really lucky the 47-bell carillon might burst your ear drums while you are up there. Probably best not to see Martin McDonagh's film *In Bruges* before the climb.

The cafes on Markt generally offer unchallenging, bland beers from global corporations. However, Panier d'Or is unusual in offering draught **Pauwel Kwak** (8%) from the Bosteels brewery, served in the unique round-bottomed coachman's glass with wooden stand that made its name. The beer is a malty amber ale that errs on the side of sweetness.

61 Parazzar
10 Tourhoutsesteenweg
T 050 33 55 28
www.parazzar.be
⊗ Shut Wednesday
🕐 17.00 til late
🍷 24
🍴 Bar snacks and meals, croques, tapas, anchovies and changing suggestions.

This new addition to the Bruges café scene opened in April 2008 though its roots go back to the European beer revival's earliest days.

Back in 1972 jazz enthusiast Tony Hostens ran a well-known bar called the Heidelberg, on Tourhoutsesteenweg in the suburban village of Loppem, west of Bruges. This was the first ever bar to sell Westmalle Dubbel on draught. It was so popular that it had to be delivered in 50 litre barrels. When Chimay wanted to offer their blond Trappist beer on tap they asked Tony to test it out first.

Tony died a couple of years ago, but now son Joeli is continuing the tradition of running a jazz café selling Trappist beer on another Tourhoutsesteenweg, the road out of town that begins at 't Zand as Smedenstraat.

His 'Soulbar' is attractively decorated with multifarious panels of loud wallpaper on dark red walls, reminiscent of a samples shop. It is furnished with handsome tables, throne-like chairs and interesting artwork. And a glitter ball.

There is table service until 22.00 after which service is at the bar. Music is jazzy and can extend to jazz does *Creep* by Radiohead. No, really.

The world's newest Trappist brewery is at Achel, bang on the Dutch border at the northernmost tip of Limburg province. Its brewhouse opened in 1998, when it joined the exclusive group of brewers who make beer that can be sold as an Authentic Trappist Product.

Achelse Kluis Trappist Achel Blond (8%) is an approachable straw-coloured beer with a good hop balance, which continues to gain class with the passage of years.

Pergola

62 **Pergola** 🍷 ❌ 🍽
Steenhouwersdijk/Meestraat
T 050 44 76 50
E pergola@dieswaene.com
www.dieswaene.com
❌ Shut Tuesday evening & Wednesday
🕐 Tue 11.30–15.00; others 11.30–21.00
🍸 12
🍴 Full restaurant menu with
an array of delicate eats.

The Pergola is the café of the prestigious hotel, Die Swaene. A member of the Small Luxury Hotels of the World Group and genuinely an extremely fine small hotel, the Swan has been used as a backdrop in many films and TV productions.

Enjoy a bistro lunch, afternoon tea or an aperitif before dinner while the canal craft chug by the garden. The hotel's glass-walled conservatory bar affords views of the surrounding buildings and the well-appointed garden.

The hotel has a proper restaurant for serious dining, so the Pergola has to make do with the likes of sautéed goose liver with apple, or scallops with endive and curry sauce, followed by poached ray with capers or a civet of wild hare.

This is a classy joint with fresh flowers on the table and top class service. Beers are served with a long ceramic tray containing a selection of exotic nuts, raisins, and a variety of other crunchy appetisers.

But the point is that nowadays top hotels stock some top quality beers and here you should try the sharp but smooth **Oude Geuze Boon** (7%) brewed at the Boon brewery in Lembeek, south of Brussels. If you are ever choosing a gueuze always make sure that the one you select is labelled *oude* gueuze, as this designation is only permitted legally for real lambic-based beers.

This dry but mellow, unfiltered brew is at the heavier end of the lambic family. It comes in a corked and caged 37.5cl bottle and is served and presented at the Pergola with appropriate ceremony. But remember, *oude* gueuze is a drink from another dimension that happens legally to be beer.

Pietje Pek

Ⓖ **Pietje Pek** ✕
13 Sint Jakobsstraat
T 050 34 78 74
www.pietjepek.com

✕ Shut Wednesday

◐ Sun 12.00–15.00 & 17.30 til late;
others 17.30–late

🍷 5

🍴 Full restaurant menu, including regional
Flemish cooking and fondues.

This popular restaurant, not too far off Markt, has disabled facilities and is family-friendly. While younger ones are helping Jonas the rabbit find his way through the maze to the carrot, you can peruse the menus on the large blackboards, which your waiter will bring to your table in your preferred language.

The menu majors in fine Flemish cuisine. Why not try the North Sea shrimp croquettes as a starter, followed by a chicken or fish *waterzooi*, *Vlaamse carbonnade* (Flemish beef stew) or wild Cabourg rabbit, hopefully no relative of Jonas, marinated in Westmalle Dubbel.

Pietje Pek is also known for its fondues with steak, veal and turkey, and its Swiss cheese fondue featuring a vat of melted Emmental, Gruyère, white wine and herbs with a dash of Kirsch and smoked ham on the side.

Although it is not as exclusive to the restaurant as they suggest, Pietje Pek is one of very few places in the city to serve **Westmalle Dubbel** (7%) on draught. The abbey at Westmalle, east of Antwerp, houses one of the most commercially adept of the Flemish Trappist breweries and its reddish-brown, full, fruity ale is one to be praised.

Poatersgat

64 Poatersgat
82 Vlamingstraat
T 0474 74 42 93
http://users.telenet.be/dauwpieter/
Open all week
17.00 til late
110
Bar snacks, lasagne, tapas.

The Monks Hole is a great new addition to the Bruges beer landscape.

What an odd bar this is. Housed in a vaulted brick cellar, it is a huge cavernous underground space. The entire floor is covered in white marble slabs – a long and expensive job for a previous owner. The ceilings are low, propped up here and there with stone columns, lit with blue halogen lights.

The combination of pale floors, stonework, low light levels and flickering candlelight at all times give the place a cool, sepulchral air, reminiscent of a crypt, but the effect is relieved by red rugs and carpets dotted here and there and by being handsomely dressed with comfy chairs and sofas.

When it is full of chattering drinkers, the gloom disappears and you may marvel at how all this is managed without need of mock-Gothic paraphernalia or plastic skulls, just a fine building and dramatic lighting.

The beer list is out of this world and is enough to wake the dead. It is not only lengthier than most, but is expertly picked, with lots of microbreweries, new Flemish brewers and a good sprinkling of Wallonian beers too. You can find Gauloise, Zinnebir, Bon Secours, Hopsinjoor, Avec Les Bons Voeux, Montagnarde, Hanssens Oude Gueuze, La Divine and others from Silly brewery. Prices are pretty good too.

One stand-out from a plethora of stand-outs is **Caracole Ambrée** (8%) from the Caracole (or Snail) brewery south of Namur, taking its name from the symbol of that city of laid back, or just plain slow people, where it was first brewed. This is a beautifully balanced amber ale with touches of caramel and toffee, in a bottle that has a label as beautifully designed as its beer.

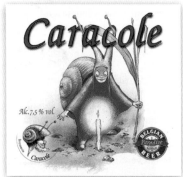

⑥⑤ Republiek 🍺 ❌
36 Sint Jakobsstraat
T 050 34 02 29
E info@derepubliek.be
www.derepubliek.be
Open all week
🕐 11.00 til late
🍸 59
🍴 Full restauarant menu, featuring world cooking.

Students' Union meets American diner in this huge single roomed café with a raised seating stage overlooking a large walled gravel terrace set around a circular tower. The building also houses a theatre and cinema making it one of Bruges' art and cultural centres.

Relaxed but busy, with fast, efficient service, it seems to be popular with families and groups of all ages.

There is an impressive, detailed menu of international cuisine from rib-eye steaks to wok-fried dishes, a fajita 'tower' and ever changing suggestions on the big blackboard.

There are plenty of new world wines and cocktails, but come here for the well above-average beer list. Amongst the small selection of lambic beers you will find one of Frank Boon's masterpieces.

Frank has been brewing at Lembeek, south of Brussels since 1990, having become a gueuze blender in 1977. Thirty years on he is one of the small number of lambic brewers who have turned round the fortunes of these remarkable drinks and forged a future for them.

The least shocking and most entertaining type of lambic are those dry, spritzy, beers called *oude kriek*, which have whole cherries steeped in them for six months before bottling. **Oude Kriek Boon** (6.5%) is a classic example, deep

red in colour, characteristically dry and sour but with the high cherry content taking away the intense sharpness that can intimidate drinkers the first time.

66 Ryad ✕
32 Hoogstraat
T 050 33 13 55
www.ryad.be
Open all week
🕛 Mon–Thu 12.00–14.30 & 18.00–22.30;
Fri–Sun 18.00–23.00
🍷 6
🍽 Full restaurant meals.

This excellent restaurant opened in 2005 to serve Moroccan and Indian food as a welcome addition to Bruges' relatively limited exotic food scene.

Inside is a two-storey fusion of North African and Bruges merchants' house, which works well. The décor is peaceful and charmingly appointed with plain washed walls, beautiful photo artwork, palm trees, Moorish lanterns, and coloured glass panels in the front window. Upstairs is a cosy, dark lounging area with brass tray-top tables, low seating and cushions for tea drinking and chicha.

As far as we are aware the roof stays shut, unlike in a real Moroccan ryad. Probably best with the North Sea only a few kilometres away.

The food makes an interesting change from the ubiquitous Flemish cuisine that Bruges does so well, with a menu offering samosas, couscous, curries and tagines.

The most interesting beer served here is **Blanche du Hainaut Biologique** (5.5%), a Bio white beer from Dupont brewery, whose impressive modern brewhouse is housed within an ancient farm in the village of Tourpes, between Tournai and Mons. The beer was launched in 1999. The wheat, barley, hops, coriander and orange peel from which it is made are all organic.

Its classical spicy, citrus flavours make this refreshing light beer a good aperitif or an appropriate accompaniment to a well-cooked tagine.

Snuffel 🍷 🥪

47–49 Ezelstraat

T 050 33 31 33

E info@snuffel.be

www.snuffel.be

Open all week

🍷 10.00 til late

🍷 25

🍽 Toasties.

Snuffel is a travellers hostel that, together with Bauhaus (above) is on the backpacker's trail. A great source of information exchange for fellow world travellers.

They claim to have the cheapest everything in town – beds, beer, bikes and internet access.

The bar, which doubles as the hostel reception is small and basic, decorated with posters of bands and music events. The obligatory collection of banknotes also makes an appearance. Music is wide-ranging and not over-loud.

They have a choice of thirty board games. The internet corner and travellers library are well-used. If you are reading this book there, don't go running off with it, OK – better buy one from behind the bar. English newspapers and magazines can also be found.

Food is minimal. Fair trade coffee and tea from Oxfam is available as are their two beers.

The beer list is on a board behind the bar and features **Delirium Tremens** (9%) the flagship beer of the Huyghe brewery near Ghent. Try to ignore the jokey pack-aging, the stone-effect bottle with a pink elephant on the label, dancing crocodiles and dragons on a balancing ball.

This is quite a serious beer full of fruit and heavy spice flavours and a warming, long, sweet afterglow. And if you do see pink elephants the next day, consider it your last beer, ever.

Speelmanshuis

68 **Speelmanshuis**
3 't Zand
⊗ Shut Monday & Thursday
Tue, Wed, Fri, Sun 14.00 til late;
Sat 09.30 til late
🍷 29
🍴 Cheese and salami plates.

The Musician's or Fiddler's House is on the shorter side of 't Zand opposite the big red terracotta concert hall, the Concertgebouw.

It is a busy little place, popular with tourists and locals, especially on Saturdays when an open market is held on the square. Most cafés overlooking the weekly market, including this one, open early on market days.

When you find customers parked on stools round the bar it is a reasonable indicator that the café appeals to locals rather than a more touristic clientele.

There is a smallish main bar room and another area down a short flight of steps, overlooking Speelmansrei canal, after which this establishment is named.

This café has a modest beer list, but has possibly the most helpful menu in Bruges, giving pictures of everything they sell. There are not only photos of the beers and soft drinks but for those whose grasp of Flemish Dutch is at the earliest stage of study, there is a picture of a plate of cheese too.

The beer we feature here is one of Belgium's biggest, though it comes in small bottles. The mighty **Bush Ambrée** (12%) is from the Dubuisson family brewery, between Tournai and Mons. This is a huge, hearty barley wine made in the English style of the 1930s. Amber in colour, it is a sweet sipping beer that warms all the way down – a perfect nightcap.

More than two and you will need those pictures to point at, including one for 'bill please'.

69 Stokershuis 🍷
  7 Langestraat
T 050 33 55 88
⊗ Shut Wednesday
🍷 18.30 til late
🍷 27
🍴 Pastas and light snacks.

When in 1985 the West Flanders tourist authorities invited the first ever party of British beer writers to Bruges, they took them to only two cafés. The Brugs Beertje for the beer, and here, the Distiller's House, for the ambience.

This small one-roomed café has changed hands a couple of times since then but retains its most traditional but unstrained Flemish feel. Candles light up the panelled walls, decorated with Delft tiles and local artwork. The attractive stone fireplace is typically Brugean, with husband and wife heads at each end, holding up the mantelpiece. The friendly owner retains a loyal local clientele, lending his dark little evening café a relaxed and cosy ambiance.

Food extends to pasta (it is famous for its spaghetti) but primarily this is a place for liquid refreshment. This includes, as you would expect, a good selection of genevers, the Belgian form of what the Dutch call *jenever*, the French *genièvre* and the English gin.

There are also three beers from the Liefmans range, paper-wrapped in corked 37.5cl bottles. The one that does not contain fruit is **Goudenband** (8%), the beer that above all others will be the barometer of the future of Belgian brewing.

Liefmans had made brown ales at Oudenaarde in East Flanders since the 17th century before takeover in the mid-Nineties led to brewery closure and a time in the doldrums.

Goudenband used to be made from a blend of freshly made brown ale with older brown beer that had been ageing in the brewery cellars for a year or more. With the closure of the brewery the beer became a brand sold on the strength of its glorious past but little more than a pastiche of its old self.

The company that had taken over sold up to new owners in 2004 but they went into liquidation in 2007. Duvel Moortgat bought most of the assets.

Takeovers are generally bad for beer quality but Duvel Moortgat have done well so far at Achouffe, which they bought in 2006. There are rumours flying around that they would even like to rebuild a brewery in Oudenaarde. Time will tell.

Goudenband is a dark reddish-brown beer that tastes slightly caramelled with some fruity tartness in the background. It has the thirst-quenching qualities common to all oak-aged Flemish brown beers and in its original form was a world classic.

Strijdershuis

70 **Strijdershuis**
14 Hallestraat
T 050 61 62 60
Open all week
Fri & Sat 10.00–1.00; others 10.00–24.00
40
Full restaurant menu including
a modern take on Flemish cuisine.

The Fighter's House is on the corner of Oude Burg and Hall-estraat, to the right side of the Belfry as you face it from Markt. The people in charge also own the Koffieboontje Hotel, the Witte Raaf restaurant and the bicycle hire shop in the same street.

This spacious and attractive modern two-storey café, with its outside terrace raised above street level, opened in 2002, eschewing all attempts to do 21st century Baroque, though there are vague Art Deco references here and there.

The food is varied and great quality, with lots of reasonably priced daily specials. We have found the scampi in cream sauce, duck breast with vegetables and various versions of mussels all outstanding.

The beer list concentrates on specific breweries. Tempting though the full range of de Dolle Brouwers' beers are, we have chosen one from another of West Flanders' well respected family breweries, Strubbe.

Keyte Ostêns Belegeringsbier (7.5%), until recently just known as Keyte (pronounced as 'cater'), has an interesting history. It was originally commissioned by Ostend beer lovers' group, De Oostendse Bierjutters, for the 400th anniversary of the ending of the Spanish siege of Ostend in 1604. This was the longest of Ostend's many sieges and the bloodiest episode of the Eighty Years' War. Although the Spanish 'won' they suffered 60,000 casualties and the Ostenders nearly as many. 'Keyte' is West Flanders dialect for, "We're even".

The beer is a golden blond which has some spicy hints, citrus and sweet tropical fruit flavours, balanced out by a good hop bitterness. It is a great drinking beer for such a significant strength.

71 Terrastje
45 Genthof
T 050 33 09 19
⊗ Shut Wednesday & Thursday
🕐 10.30–23.30
🍺 40
🍽 Flemish meals a speciality.

The Little Terrace is a little gem. Only two hundred metres off the beaten track but this is far enough away from the summer hordes, particularly at weekends, to reward the extra trek.

It gets its name from the pleasant wooden-decked area at the front from which you can get a good view of the canal, where cormorants can often be seen fishing for eel or perching on wooden posts sticking up from the water, hanging their wings out to dry.

This small one-roomed cafe has friendly service and while it would be wrong to describe it as a restaurant, they do cook traditional regional main courses and make waffles.

The beer list is more imaginative than most. They also have a beer of the month that tends to promote stronger beers and those from the Smisje brewery. However, uniquely for Bruges they have **Watou's Witbier** (5%) permanently on draught, from the Van Eecke brewery.

Van Eecke is most famous for its Kapittel range of abbey-style beers and the hop-laden Poperings Hommelbier. Watou's Witbier, their light, cloudy wheat beer is said by many to be the best of its type in Belgium, with a wonderful lemon citrus and coriander flavour that is most refreshing, especially in summer.

Tijl en Nele

72 Tijl en Nele 🛒
  2 Jacob Van Maerlantstraat (Damme)
T 050 35 71 92
E tijl.nele@pandora.be
  www.tijlennele.com
⊗ Shut Thu & Fri (Nov–Easter); Fri (Easter–Nov)
🕐 Mon–Fri 09.30–18.00; Sat & Sun 09.00–18.00.
  July & Aug open all day
🍷 12
🥪 Sandwiches to take away.

Damme's economic survival in the 21st century depends on preserving its image as the place that inspired much of Flemish literature. In particular, the work of Charles De Coster, who in 1867 published *The Legend of Thyl Ulenspiegel and Lamme Goedzak*, the stories of legendary young joker Tijl, his friend Lamme and girlfriend Nele. The Tijl stories concentrate on the tricks he plays to rid Flanders of the Spanish occupation. And of course, in the end, no longer the fool, Tijl becomes the hero.

The modern incarnation of Tijl en Nele in their home town is a pretty little shop that specialises in local food and drink, bicycle hire and sandwiches.

The selection of beers in the shop have been chosen for their local links, though Pater Van Damme Bruin (8%) is nowadays the excellent **Potteloereke** (8%) from tiny microbrewery Sint Canarus of Gottem in East Flanders, rebadged with a local name.

It can be drunk from special pottery mugs that can also be bought in the shop and which hark back to the commissioning of the 'mother' beer by two local potters who work near the brewery and make the pots that Sint Canarus beers are often served from.

It is a confident, mature, darkish, red-brown strong ale which has a spiced and caramel taste, a touch of liquorice and a warming finish. Thoroughly recommended.

Tuf Tuf

73 Tuf Tuf
1 Ketsbruggestraat
T 050 38 17 87
⊗ Shut Monday & Tuesday
🌙 Sun 11.00–22.00; Wed & Thu 11.00–20.00;
Fri & Sat 11.00–23.00
🍷 19
🍴 Light snacks.

This wide-windowed, high set bar gets its name from the fact that it overlooks the station, which is also the transport hub of Bruges. With apologies in advance to all but young English children, it translates into English as chuff-chuff.

This is a great waiting room from which to watch Bruges on the move and a good first and last café stop if you are coming and going via the station, its bus stops or any of its car parks.

Tuf Tuf is also handy for the shows set up on the square in front of the station at various times throughout the year, the most notable of which is the fantastic Snow and Ice Exhibition, running from November to New Year.

The café has a wide variety of small snacks to keep you going. With each beer they serve a sizable bowl of remarkably orange-coloured crisps.

This is one of the few bars in the city that serves the flagship beer from Antwerp's De Koninck brewery on draught. Officially **De Koninck Amber** (5%) nowadays, it is still better known as De Koninck. If you are confident with your Dutch, try ordering it in the manner of a native Antwerper, who would simply ask for a *bolleke* (try boll-a-ker), the name of its stemmed glass.

This wonderfully straightforward, rounded lightish pale ale just begs you to order another.

74 Verloren Hoek
178 Carmersstraat
T 050 33 06 98
⊗ Shut Tuesday & Wednesday
🍺 Sat 10.30–14.00 & 17.00 til late;
others 10.30 til late
🍷 15
🍽 Home-made meals, includes steaks and fish
(Thu–Mon 12.00–14.00 & 18.00–21.00).

The Lost Corner is set just within the city's ring road opposite one of the two huge working windmills to have survived after the burgers took the brave decision in the late Sixties to take down most of the old city walls in order to preserve the city's old centre.

The windmills' roles had been to harness the wind in order to pump water and grind corn, being generally eco-friendly in a remarkably futuristic way. They are open to visitors every day in summer. Tourists rarely venture this far out of the centre. It looks a long way on a map but central Bruges is smaller than any map suggests and a visit here and to the Windmolen (below) is well worth considering.

This small, family-run tavern is busy mainly with local Brugeans, especially on a Sunday. One of the reasons is its excellent food, all home-prepared, on an interesting and ever-changing menu, in generous portions and at non-tourist prices.

They also have private accommodation for rent.

The small beer list includes **Brugse Zot Dubbel** (7.5%), big sister to the more readily available blond beer from the city's Halve Maan brewery. Still developing, it has a rich ruby brown colour and there are smooth sweet roast malt flavours that make it an appealing choice. It's on draught here.

Verdi

 Verdi
5 Vlamingstraat
T 050 34 42 43
www.verdibrugge.com
Shut Monday evening & Tuesday
Mon 09.00–18.00; Wed 08.00–22.00;
Thu–Sun 09.00–22.00
30
Full restaurant meals and snacks,
also a tearoom.

Verdi is big, not just in physical presence but also in concept. Just round the corner from the north side of Markt and named in honour of the great Italian composer Guiseppe Verdi, this place seems to have acquired a job lot of small busts of the great man as the little white heads are in evidence everywhere.

On entering there is a pretty tearoom to the left, with a larger salon that doubles as a restaurant and tearoom straight ahead. All rooms are comfortable and appointed in what the owners term Venetian-Spanish-English influence. To increase the international flavour, the food is classic Franco-Belgian.

They serve freshly made waffles and pancakes every day except Thursdays. While away the time in this relaxed place with a waffle and play spot the Verdi.

The beer we suggest you try here is **Liefmans Kriekbier** (6%), now brewed by Duvel Moortgat. This is not historically a cherry lambic but rather a brown ale in which whole cherries were steeped. Although slightly sweet, it is not overly so.

This has been a beer in transition for some while, since the

Liefmans brewery in Oudenaarde closed more than a decade ago. What Duvel Moortgat do with it will be interesting but the early signs are that they would like to return it to being one of the country's finest fruit beers, in a sharpish fruity style largely its own and not one of the syrupy ones.

76 Vino Vino
15 Grauwwerkersstraat
T 050 34 51 15
⊗ Shut Sunday & Monday from 12.00
🕐 Tue–Thu 18.00–24.00; Fri&Sat 18.00–01.00
🍷 18
🍴 Tapas and bar meals.

This pleasant evening haunt is another bar whose outside, especially when shut, does not do justice to its inside. Suggesting that it only sells wine does not help either.

On a quiet street that links St Jakobstraat and Vlamingstraat, slightly off the main drag north of Markt, this is a 'Blues and Tapas bar', with a tiled terracotta floor, dark wood ceiling and matching furniture. Decorated with Rioja bottles and always candlelit, it makes a relaxed hideaway.

The outstanding beer on the menu is **St Bernardus Tripel** (8%) from Sint-Bernard of Watou. The brewery was originally set up in 1946 to brew imitation Trappist beers under licence from the monks of St Sixtus' abbey at Westvleteren, which did not have the capacity to go commercial in any serious way.

In 1992 the Abbey ended the licensing agreement and left the brewery without its brands. Bravely, they responded by improving the existing imitations and adding some new beers. Tripel was the first of these and became an instant success, giving the Trappist breweries a run for their money by creating a beer with an excellent balance of malt and hop character.

The brewery's tag line is *"Hemelse nectar binnen handbereik"*, or heavenly nectar within reach. Is it just us, or is that a gentle dig? It is on draught here. Marvellous.

77 Vlissinghe
2 Blekersstraat
T 050 34 37 37
E info@cafevlissinghe.be
www.cafevlissinghe.be
⊗ Shut Monday & Tuesday
🕑 Sun 10.00–19.00;
Wed & Thu 11.00–24.00;
Fri & Sat 11.00 til late
🍷 25
🍴 Light snacks.

Vlissinghe is one of Bruges' great old buildings but a little off the beaten track.

It is the oldest continuously licensed premises in the city, having functioned as some form of café, tavern or hostelry since 1515. The interior impresses with its mighty wooden tables, heavily studded chairs, polished copper, copious brassware and porcelain, with the walls covered in *oude* Brugge artwork, maps, portraits and heraldic things. The room is dominated by one of the best and largest old Brugean stoves we have encountered.

Outside at the rear is a lovely garden with a pitch on which to play petanque *(boules)*. Inside are board games for the less energetic.

Food is limited to pastas, croques, soups (in winter) and the ubiquitous pancakes and ice cream.

Van Eecke brewery is found in Watou, outside Poperinge, in the heart of Belgium's main hop growing area. Despite this being one of the earliest places of hop farming, with over 700 years of continuous cultivation to date, hoppy beers have not been a major part of Flemish beer heritage.

On the beer list you will find **Poperings Hommelbier** (7.5%), one of the first hop beers to emerge in the region in recent years.

This delightful pale ale delivers hoppiness, not in the brash, outspoken manner of an American hop monster, but rather with finesse. It can be enjoyed year-round but makes a surprisingly refreshing summer beer.

Windmolen

78 Windmolen
135 Carmersstraat
T 050 33 97 39
⊗ Shut Friday evening; Sat & Sun from 15.00
🕐 10.00–22.00
🍷 19
🍴 Light snacks.

The Windmill is located just inside the ring road end of Carmersstraat, opposite the Veloren Hoek (above). This gorgeous little café has a super view of one of Bruges' working windmills. When it is operating you can enjoy a great free show. The paddles get up quite a speed and you can start to realise their power.

Against a backdrop of exposed brickwork, its lovely interior is packed with cane chairs, old enamel drinks signs, birdcages, lamps, vehicle licence plates, coffee grinders, jugs, Singer sewing machines, witches, clowns, pot plants, hop festoons and of course, windmills. Minimalist, it is not.

The menu stretches to spaghetti, other pastas and omelettes and is also big on desserts, ice-creams and milkshakes, reflecting its predominantly daytime trade.

Our featured beer here is family brewer Van Honsebrouck's **Kasteel Bruin** (11%). The various Castle Beer brands are named after Ingelmunster Castle, featured on the label, which the family bought in the 1980s. It was first produced in 1989 and is served in a handsome chalice.

The brewery is upgrading its beers at the moment. In its current form, whatever you think of this mighty ale, subtlety is not a word that comes to mind. Sweetness pervades an uncompromising experience, which some adore.

79 Zandloper 🍴 ✗
   33 't Zand
T 050 34 13 46
E roland.brackx1@telenet.be
✗ Shut Wednesday
🕐 10.00 til late
🍷 38
🍴 Full restaurant menu, with three-course
   set menus prominent.

The Hour Glass is a large, one-roomed, bright, modern café-restaurant just off 't Zand, featuring a bit more originality in its beer menu than the standard tourist fare usually found around the square.

Food-wise fish soup and proper home-made shrimp croquettes feature, together with rack of lamb, wok-fried creations and rabbit cooked in beer, along with the usual waffles, pancakes and ice cream.

In season they serve the deep, rich Corsendonk Christmas ale and year-round offer a cherry beer from Frank Boon's brewery in 37.5cl corked bottles. Other highlights on the beer menu are Bourgogne des Flandres, Delirium Tremens, and two beers from the highly respected Malheur brewery of Buggenhout, northwest of Brussels.

The Malheur 12 is their dark barley wine but here we feature the slightly lighter **Malheur 10** (10%), a hazy golden beer and this one is as full-bodied as its strength would indicate. You can taste the alcohol though it is moderated by the warming honey tastes and pronounced hoppiness in the background of this accomplished beer.

Zwarte Kat

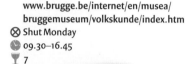

80 Zwarte Kat 🍷
43 Balstraat
T 050 44 87 64
www.brugge.be/internet/en/musea/
bruggemuseum/volkskunde/index.htm
⊗ Shut Monday
🕐 09.30–16.45
🍷 7
🍴 None.

The Black Cat is officially a museum café and you need to go into the museum to get to the bar. The maximum entrance fee is a modest €3 with even cheaper deals for young and old, including entrance packages to some of the other ten Bruggemuseum members with the same ticket.

This one is the Volkskunde or Folklore museum, housed in a row of eight 17th century low-rise whitewashed almshouses once owned by the Guild of Shoemakers. It aims to recreate life in bygone Bruges and features thematic reconstructions of old interiors filled with appropriate objects. These include a cobbler's workshop, grocery, kitchen, pharmacy, school room, milliner's workshop, confectioner

(still making great smelling fresh sweets on Thursdays) and last but not least the Black Cat café.

The interior is created from artefacts of genuine but long gone café interiors in the city, with an impressive old bar counter and grandfather clock. There is a lovely old organ that will fire up with a loud tune for a mere 20 cents coin.

The real star is the Zwarte Kat itself, which stalks the museum. The present prowler is the third in the dynasty and is fond of coffee drinkers, or more correctly their discarded milk pots. There is a collection box on the bar marked *Voor de kat*, or for the cat. It makes you wonder what he spends it on.

The beer list here is short and chalked onto a tiny black slate. One of these is **Steenbrugge Dubbel Bruin** (6.5%), one of the recently restyled, bottle-conditioned Abbey beers from Palm Brewery in Steenhuffel. It is amber brown in colour and is a light-bodied beer with fruit banana tastes, and a light, roasted malt presence.

Index of breweries and beers

Bruges is in the administrative centre for the province of West Flanders, roughly equivalent to an English county. About 30% of the beers featured in this book come from West Flanders, with the others coming from eight of the country's nine other provinces, plus one from the Netherlands.

ANTWERP

Anker, *from the city of Mechelen*
⑱ Gouden Carolus Classic (8.5%)

De Koninck, *from the city of Antwerp*
⑦ De Koninck Amber (5%)

Duvel Moortgat, *from Breendonk, SW of Antwerp*
⑯ Duvel (8.5%)
⑲ Liefmans Goudenband (8%)
⑮ Liefmans Kriekbier (6%)
❻ Maredsous Triple (10%)

Scheldebrouwerij, *from Meer, NE of Antwerp*
㊼ Lamme Goedzak (7%)

signifies a Trappist abbey brewery where brewing is overseen by monks.

Westmalle,* *from Westmalle, NE of Antwerp*
⑬ Westmalle Dubbel (7%)
㊾ Westmalle Tripel (9.5%)

EAST FLANDERS

Bosteels, *from Buggenhout, NW of Brussels*
㊵ Tripel Karmeliet (8%)
⑥ Pauwel Kwak (8%)

De Ryck, *from Herzele, SE of Ghent*
❷ Arend Dubbel (6.5%)

Huyghe, *from Melle, SE of Ghent*
㊿ Delirium Tremens (9%)
㊳ Oxfam Bruin (7.5%)

Malheur, *from Buggenhout, NW of Brussels*
⑲ Malheur 10 (10%)

Proef, *from Lochristi, NE of Ghent*
㊱ Gageleer (7%)
㊶ Vicaris Generaal (8.8%)

Roman, *from Oudenaarde, south of Ghent*
㊻ Ename Dubbel (6.5%)

Sint Canarus, *from Gottem, SW of Ghent*
⑫ Potteloereke (8%)

Slaghmuylder, *from Ninove, west of Brussels*
㊲ Witkap Stimulo (6%)

Smisje, *from Mater-Oudenaarde, south of Ghent*
㉝ Guido (8%)
⑮ Smisje Dubbel (9%)

Van Steenberge, *from Ertvelde, north of Ghent*
㉖ Augustijn (aged) (8%)
㊽ Gulden Draak (10.5%)

FLEMISH BRABANT

Boon, *from Lembeek, south of Brussels*
㊷ Oude Geuze Boon (7%)
㊺ Oude Kriek Boon (6.5%)
❹ Framboise Boon (5%)

3 Fonteinen, *from Beersel, SW of Brussels*
㊺ 3 Fonteinen Oude Geuze (6%)

Haacht, *from Bortmeerbeek, NE of Brussels*
⑩ Adler (6.5%)
❼ Gildenbier (7%)

Hanssens, *from Dworp, SW of Brussels*
❺ Hanssens Artisanaal Oude Kriek (6%)

Palm, *from Steenhuffel, NW of Brussels*
❾ Brugge Tripel (8.2%)
⑳ Steenbrugge Dubbel Bruin (6.5%)
㉑ Steenbrugge Wit (5%)

Timmermans, *from Vlezenbeek, west of Brussels*
⑲ Bourgogne des Flandres (5%)

HAINAUT

Abbaye des Rocs, *from Montignies-sur-Roc, SW of Mons*
❶ Abbaye des Rocs (9%)

Chimay,* *from Scourmont, south of Charleroi*
㉛ Chimay Grande Reserve (Bleue) (9%)

Index of breweries and beers

Dubuisson, *from Pipaix, east of Tournai*
68 Bush Ambrée (12%)
21 Cuvée des Trolls (7%)

Dupont, *from Tourpes, east of Tournai*
14 Biolégère (3.5%)
66 Blanche du Hainaut Biologique (5.5%)
52 Saison Dupont (6.5%)

Écaussinnes, *from Ecaussinnes, NE of Mons*
20 Cookie Beer (8%)

Legendes (des), *from Ellezelles, NE of Tournai*
42 Hercule Stout (9%)

Ranke (de), *from Dottignies, south of Kortrijk*
32 XX Bitter (6.2%)

LIMBURG

Achel, *from Achel on the Dutch border*
61 Trappist Achel Blond (8%)
54 Trappist Achel Bruin (8%)

LUXEMBOURG

Achouffe, *from Achouffe, near Houffalize*
30 La Chouffe (8%)

Orval, *from Villers-devant-Orval, near Florenville*
43 Orval (6.2%)

Rulles, *from Rulles, west of Arlon*
17 La Rulles Estivale (5.2%)

NAMUR

Bocq (du), *from Purnode, south of Namur*
34 Ramée Blonde (8%)

Caracole, *from Falmignoul, south of Dinant*
64 Caracole Ambree (8%)

Rochefort, *from Rochefort, SE of Namur*
3 Rochefort 8 (9.2%)
12 Rochefort 10 (11.3%)

WALLONIAN BRABANT

Lefèbvre, *from Quenast, SW of Brussels*
25 Barbār (8%)
57 Floreffe Prima Melior (8%)

WEST FLANDERS

Alvinne, *from Heule, north of Kortrijk*
24 Alvinne Extra Restyled (7%)
8 Podge Belgian Imperial Stout (10.5%)

Bavik, *from Bavikhove, NE of Kortrijk*
29 Ezel Bruin (6.5%)
36 Petrus Oud Bruin (5.5%)
53 Pilaarbijter Blond (7.2%)

De Leite, *from Ruddervoorde, south of Bruges*
11 Femme Fatale (6.5%)

Deca, *from Woesten, near the French border*
28 Pannepøt (10%)

Dolle Brouwers, *from Esen, SW of Bruges*
13 Oerbier (9%)

Halve Maan, *from the city of Bruges*
37 Brugse Zot Blond (6%)
74 Brugse Zot Dubbel (7.5%)

Rodenbach, *from Roeselare, SW of Bruges*
39 Rodenbach (5.2%)

Sint-Bernard, *from Watou, near the French border*
35 St Bernardus Abt 12 (10.5%)
59 St Bernardus Prior 8 (8%)
76 St Bernardus Tripel (8%)

Strubbe, *from Ichtegem, SW of Bruges*
44 Ichtegem's Oud Bruin (5%)
70 Keyte Ostêns Belegeringsbier (7.5%)

Van Eecke, *from Watou, near the French border*
77 Poperings Hommelbier (7.5%)
71 Watou's Witbier (5%)
55 Kapittel Abt (10%)

Van Honsebrouck, *from Ingelmunster, north of Kortrijk*
23 Brigand (9%)
50 Kasteel Triple (11%)
78 Kasteel Bruin (11%)

Verhaeghe, *from Vichte, east of Kortrijk*
22 Duchesse de Bourgogne (6.2%)

THE NETHERLANDS

Koningshoeven, *from east of Tilburg*
38 La Trappe Quadrupel (10%)

94

Podge's Belgian Beer Tours

Tours taking in the most innovative of

Belgium's breweries, festivals and beer cafes.

See **www.podgebeer.co.uk**

or ring **01245 354677** for details

 **podge**

Driving people to drink since 1994